a new introduction to
GEOGRAPHY
for OCR GCSE Specification A
REVISION GUIDE

Written by: John Belfield, Steve Sibley, Greg Hart
Edited by: Keith Flinders

The publishers would like to thank the following individuals, institutions and companies for permission to reproduce copyright illustrations in this book:

John Maier/Still Pictures: page 31; © Mike McQueen/CORBIS: page 48 (right); John Belfield: pages 32, 48 (top left, middle and bottom), 62; Steve Sibley: pages 46, 66, 69; Keith Flinders: page 68 (left) University of Hull: page 68 (right); Ordnance Survey mapping on behalf of The Controller of Her Majesty's Stationery Office, Crown Copyright MC.

Hodder Headline's policy is to use papers that are natural, renewable and recyclable products and made from wood grown in sustainable forests. The logging and manufacturing processes are expected to conform to the environmental regulations of the country of origin.

Every effort has been made to trace and acknowledge ownership of copyright. The publishers will be glad to make suitable arrangements with any copyright holders whom it has not been possible to contact.

Note about the Internet links in the book. The user should be aware that URLs or web addresses change regularly. Every effort has been made to ensure the accuracy of the URLs provided in this book on going to press. It is inevitable, however, that some will change. It is sometimes possible to find a relocated web page, by just typing in the address of the home page for a website in the URL window of your browser.

Orders: please contact Bookpoint Ltd, 130 Milton Park, Abingdon, Oxon OX14 4SB. Telephone: (44) 01235 827720. Fax: (44) 01235 400454. Lines are open from 9.00 - 6.00, Monday to Saturday, with a 24 hour message answering service. You can also order through our website www.hodderheadline.co.uk.

British Library Cataloguing in Publication Data
A catalogue record for this title is available from the British Library

ISBN -10: 0 340 876 433
ISBN -: 978 0 340 87643 5

First Published 2004

Impression number   10 9 8 7 6 5 4 3 2
Year   2010 2009 2008 2007 2006 2005

Copyright © 2004 John Belfield, Keith Flinders, Greg Hart, Steve Sibley.

All rights reserved. No part of this publication may be reproduced or transmitted in any form or by any means, electronic or mechanical, including photocopy, recording, or any information storage and retrieval system, without permission in writing from the publisher or under licence from the Copyright Licensing Agency Limited. Further details of such licences (for reprographic reproduction) may be obtained from the Copyright Licensing Agency Limited, of 90 Tottenham Court Road, London W1T 4LP.

Typeset by Pantek Arts Ltd, Maidstone, Kent.
Printed in Great Britain for Hodder Education, a division of Hodder Headline, 338 Euston Road, London NW1 3BH by Hobbs The Printers, Totton, Hants.

contents

INTRODUCTION	2
Knowing where to begin	2
LEARNING TO LEARN	4
1. Learning Facts and Details	4
2. Getting Organised	7
3. Thinking Things Through	9
UNIT 1 PEOPLE AND THE PHYSICAL WORLD	12
Plate Tectonics	12
Rivers	13
Coasts	15
A detailed look at one question	16
Case study answers	18
UNIT 2 PEOPLE AND PLACES TO LIVE	22
Population	22
Settlement	24
Different types of questions	27
How the examiners award the marks	30
Case study answers	33
UNIT 3 PEOPLE AND THEIR NEEDS	38
Quality of Life	38
Economic Activities	40
Energy	42
Case study answers	43
Different Types of Resources	46
UNIT 4 PEOPLE AND THE ENVIRONMENT	50
Local Environment	50
Global Environment	53
How the case study is marked	56
HOW TO PREPARE FOR PAPERS 3 AND 4	58
Checklist	70

introduction

It's exam day. You set off for school in good time. You feel confident, because you know you have done the work. You have revised thoroughly and effectively. You know how the question paper will be laid out. You know the style of the questions, how many you will have to do, how much time to allow yourself and the kinds of answers you will need to produce.

This book is all about giving you that confidence. It will help you find the most appropriate way for you to revise. You will become familiar with how your examiners will try to find out how good a Geographer you really are. They are not trying to catch you out. There will be no trick questions. All the topics examined are clearly set out in the Specification (your teacher might call it the syllabus). It's not a secret document. You can download your own copy from the internet. You'll find it at www.ocr.org.uk. (If you are taking the GCSE Short Course, it is Specification 1086 instead of 1986)

The Specification tells you very clearly what you need to study to do well.

- It tells you at what scale you should study it. UK means within the United Kingdom. EU stands for European Union (but note that in this course, EU means the rest of the European Union and does **not include UK**). The places you have studied are at different stages of development. Some you may have called 'Third World'. In GCSE Geography, they are Less Economically Developed Countries (LEDCs). Other places are More Economically Developed Countries (MEDCs). You can use the initials LEDC and MEDC in your exam answers. You don't need to write out the words. It is not a simple split like sheep and goats. Some countries are not easy to classify. If you are answering an exam question about development, your examiner is aware that most countries are not at one extreme or the other – and that within some LEDCs, there are areas of strong economic development and wealth; most MEDCs have areas of poor development and poverty too. The Specification identifies those parts of the course which must be set in LEDCs and which in MEDCs.

- The Specification shows the content on four double page spreads, one for each unit. You will see the columns showing scale to the left and context (where) to the right. A tick means it must be included in your Geography course; a + means there is a choice.

- The column on the right hand edge gives information such as possible case studies. Where the writing is in italics, it is only a suggestion, so don't worry if you have studied a different case study. Just make sure you know which one you did instead!

The details in the Specification were written for teachers. If you are concerned by anything there that you don't understand, ask your teacher to explain it to you. It is most important that you go into the exam confident that you know what is required of you.

You have two exam papers. The first is 2 hours long. A few days later, the other exam paper is 1 hour. You will be entered for the exams at either **Foundation Tier** or **Higher Tier**. It is important that you are entered for the most appropriate tier. Don't expect to get the grade that best shows your talent at Geography if the questions are too difficult to understand, or so easy that you don't have to try very hard. Foundation Tier has Papers 1 and 3; Higher Tier has Papers 2 and 4. Both tiers award Grades C and D. Higher Tier also asks questions to find out if you are worth Grades A*, A and B. Foundation Tier also includes Grades E, F and G. It is important to realise that it is the same Geography whichever tier you take.

The Specification groups together the work which makes up your GCSE Geography course into four Units. These are:

Unit 1 People and the Physical World
Unit 2 People and Places to Live
Unit 3 People and their Needs
Unit 4 People and the Environment

Paper 1 and **Paper 2** have questions about all four Units so you will need to revise them all.

A New Introduction to Geography for OCR GCSE Specification A: Revision Guide

FIGURE 1

An example of the Specification Grid

Population	Scale				Context					The following is amplification including some possible exemplars of case studies that could be included in a programme of study sfor this specification.
	Small/ Local	Regional/ National	International/ Global	Unspecified	MEDC			LEDC	Unspecified	
					UK	EU	Other			**Population**
(a) Factors affecting the density and distribution of population.	+	+	✓						✓	(a) Physical, economic and social factors, with reference to an area of high density and an area of low density population.
(b) Variations in population structure between countries.		✓			+	+	+		✓	(b) Population pyramids. Implications of the proportion of population in young, adult and elderly group. Dependent population.
(c) The causes and consequences of population change.		✓	✓		+	+	+		✓	(c) Birth rate, death rate and international migration; a case study of strategies to influence population change, e.g. *China's one child policy*; importance of values and attitudes. A case study of international migration e.g. *Mexicans to USA*.
Settlement										**Settlement**
(a) Causes and consequences of rural to urban migration. Strategies to improve the quality of life and improve sustainability in squatter settlements.		✓	✓					✓		(a) A case study to illustrate 'Push' and 'Pull' factors, the effects on rural areas, shanty town development. The significance and effects of the attitudes and values of those involved, e.g. *migration into Bangladesh's cities or from North East Brazil to the cities of the South East*
(b) The characteristics of land use zones in urban areas.	✓				✓					(b) A case study of an urban area to illustrate the characteristics of the central business district, inner zones and outer suburbs, the rural/urban fringe e.g. *Swansea*.
(c) Strategies to improve the quality of life in urban areas.	✓	✓			+	+	+			(c) How considerations of sustainable development affect planning and management. A case study of urban traffic management e.g. *transport planning in Glasgow* and one case study of urban regeneration e.g. *Swansea*.
(d) Provision of services in urban and rural areas.	✓	✓			+	+	+			(d) The interdependence of a town and its surrounding area to illustrate the hierarchy of settlements and services, out of town shopping centres, neighbourhood centres and service provision in villages e.g. *North Worcestershire*.
(e) Changes in rural areas.	✓	✓			✓					(e) The causes and consequences of urban to rural migration; the impact of second homes; social and economic changes to village populations; the significance and effects of the attitudes and values of those involved e.g. *North Worcestershire*.

Paper 1 has four questions, as there is one question from each Unit. Foundation Tier candidates answer all four questions. They are structured questions, so they have several parts to them. There will be several resources too. There could be a map, a graph, a short extract from a newspaper, a photograph or a cartoon. The resources are numbered according to the question they are with. So if there are three resources for Question 2, they will be Fig. 2a, Fig. 2b and Fig. 2c. Most resources are printed in the exam paper, as close as possible to the questions about them. If the resource is in colour though, it will be in a separate Resource Booklet tucked inside the exam paper. After each question, there are lines where you write your answer. (However, not all questions need a written answer. Sometimes you are asked to draw part of a graph or add something to a map.)

The next section helps you to discover how best to revise. Then from page 12 you will find out about the exam papers.

- What topics to revise.
- What types of questions to expect.
- What resources to expect with the questions.
- What the command words mean.
- How to use a writing frame to help answer case study questions.
- How the marks are allocated.

If you have the text book 'A New Introduction to Geography for OCR GCSE Specification A' you can cross reference the page number where you see ▭.

Paper 2 also has structured questions, but there are fewer short answer parts and more opportunities to write in paragraphs. For this reason, Higher Tier candidates do not answer Paper 2 in spaces on the exam paper. Instead you will use booklets of lined paper. (Make sure you remember to put your name, the number of your Examination Centre – that means your school – and your candidate number on each one.) The other big difference to Paper 1 is that you have a choice. On Paper 2, two questions are set on each of the four Units of the Specification. For each Unit you choose the one you think will give you the highest score.

Paper 3 and **Paper 4** test your skills and understanding. There are two questions (though each has several parts) and they could come from any Unit of the Specification. There will always be an Ordnance Survey map and usually other resources such as photographs or a satellite image for you to use. Unlike Paper 2, Higher Tier candidates do not use separate lined paper this time. Both Paper 3 and Paper 4 have answer lines amongst the questions, as there are often tasks to do, like drawing part of a cross section.

There is lots for you to do too.

- Revision tasks to tackle.
- Answers from candidates to think about. (The Examiner tells you the good and bad points to look out for!)
- Tips from the Examiner on how to be successful.
- 'Model' answers to show you how to do well.

Learning to Learn

Revision is part of how you learn and how you use learning to pass an exam. Exams are tests of what you know, understand and can do.

Revision begins when you start your GCSE course.

You can prepare by

- Finding out what you need to know.
- Organising your notes. Have a list of the ideas and case studies.
- Raising your awareness through TV news and newspapers.
- Finding time to reflect on each lesson and to review your work every four weeks.
- Knowing how GCSE questions are structured.
- Finding out which tier (Higher or Foundation) is best for you.

You need to think about what you are good at, what you need to improve and how you can improve.

We do not all learn in the same way. There are many ways to revise. Some people prefer lists; others use pictures and diagrams. What type of learner are you? Think how you have revised for examinations in the past. Relying on one style of learning may limit what you can achieve. Effective learners use a **range** of learning styles.

Your GCSE Geography course provides you with lots of information and develops your geographical skills. Here are ideas that help you use what you already know and increase your understanding.

They will help you to

- learn facts and details
- get organised
- think things through
- become familiar with past papers.

1. LEARNING FACTS AND DETAILS

Do you find it difficult to learn and remember lists of key words, facts and places? It helps if you can link a fact to a specific idea or example to give it meaning. This then acts as a **trigger**. A trigger is something to remind you of a specific piece of detail. Triggers help you recall selected information. Try these triggers:

- Use a visual image, such as colours or a cartoon.
- Use a sound or tune, such as a rhyme or mnemonic.

Using a visual image

Geographical ideas can often be shown more simply as a diagram. Can you complete a copy of the diagram below to show a shopping centre hierarchy? [113]

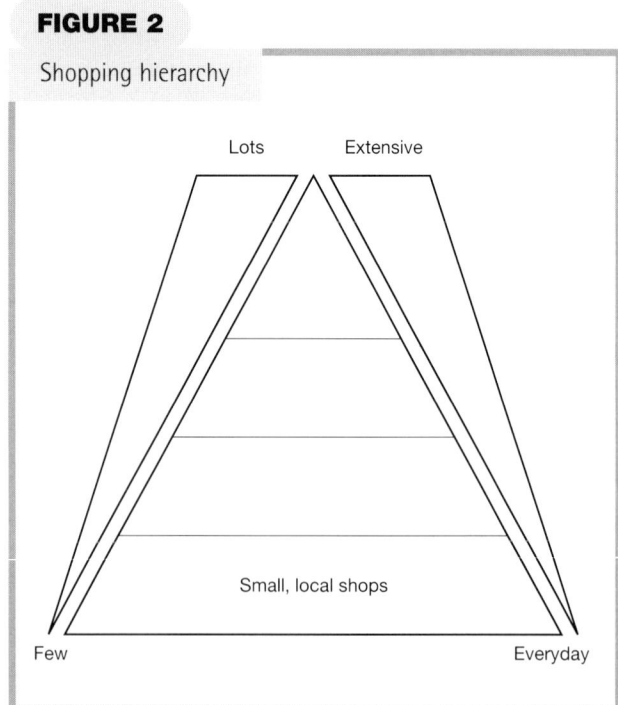

FIGURE 2
Shopping hierarchy

FIGURE 3

Rural–urban settlement hierarchy

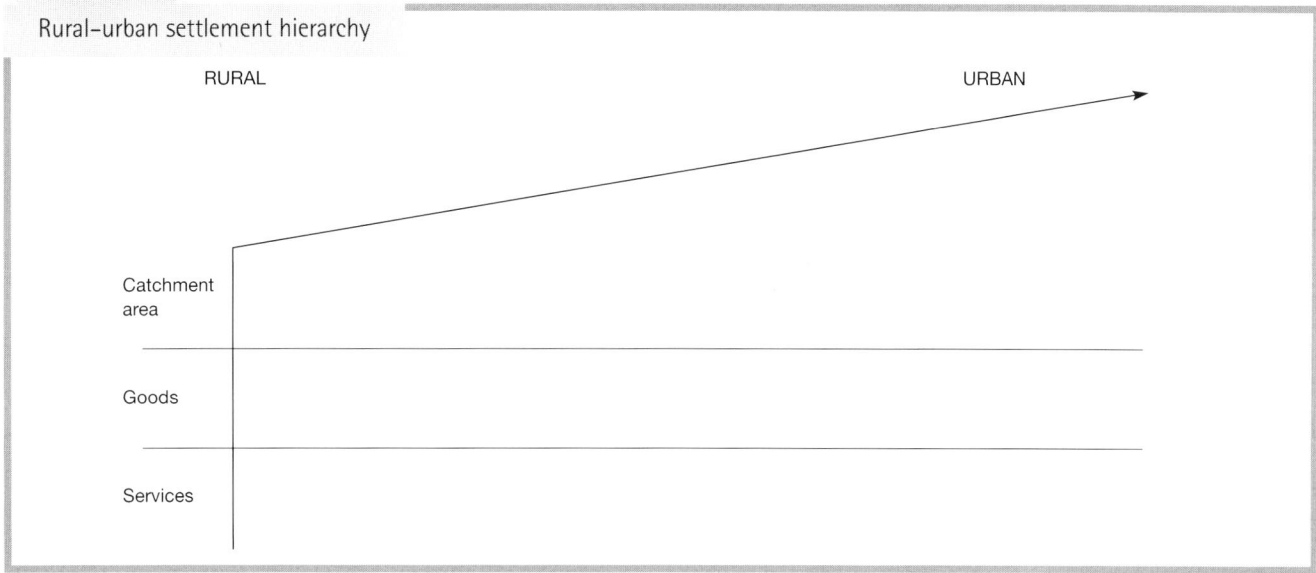

Copy the frame above. Then try to draw from memory a diagram to show the rural to urban settlement hierarchy. [📖 *100–101*]

Sometimes recalling a process in words is difficult. It may be easier to use pictures. The example below shows the formation of an ox bow lake. [📖 *31*] Draw each stage and each word box onto a separate piece of paper. To see if you understand the sequence, shuffle them then lay them out in order.

FIGURE 4

Matching label and diagram: ox bow lake

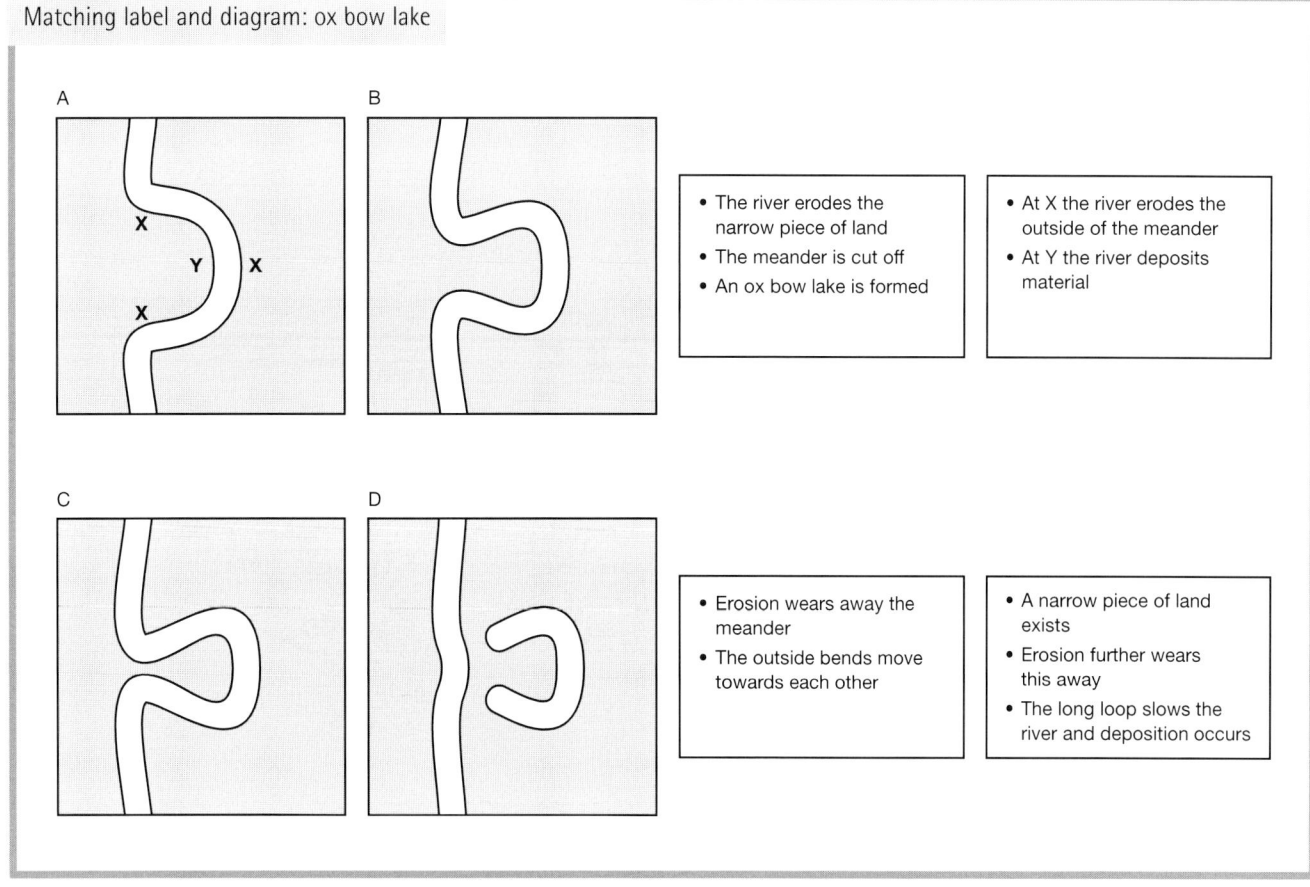

Learning to Learn

Now they show the stages in the development of an ox bow lake. Together they make sense. By adding a commentary in notes under each drawing, you can describe each stage.

Try to produce other useful images to trigger your memory and help you recall information

Destructive plate boundary [8]
Headland recession [44]
Longshore drift [46]
North–South divide [130]
Location of an industry [152]
Effects of a pit closure [165]
Consequences of deforestation [187]
Greenhouse effect [206]

Using a sound or theme

These ideas help you structure unrelated pieces of information. They create a story, with the image of each event acting as the trigger for the next. Here is an example of a story board to help you learn the process of rural to urban migration in LEDCs. [84]

FIGURE 5
Storyboard – rural–urban migration

Rural proverty. We live in …
Quality of life. Our lives are …
Expectations. We heard about … 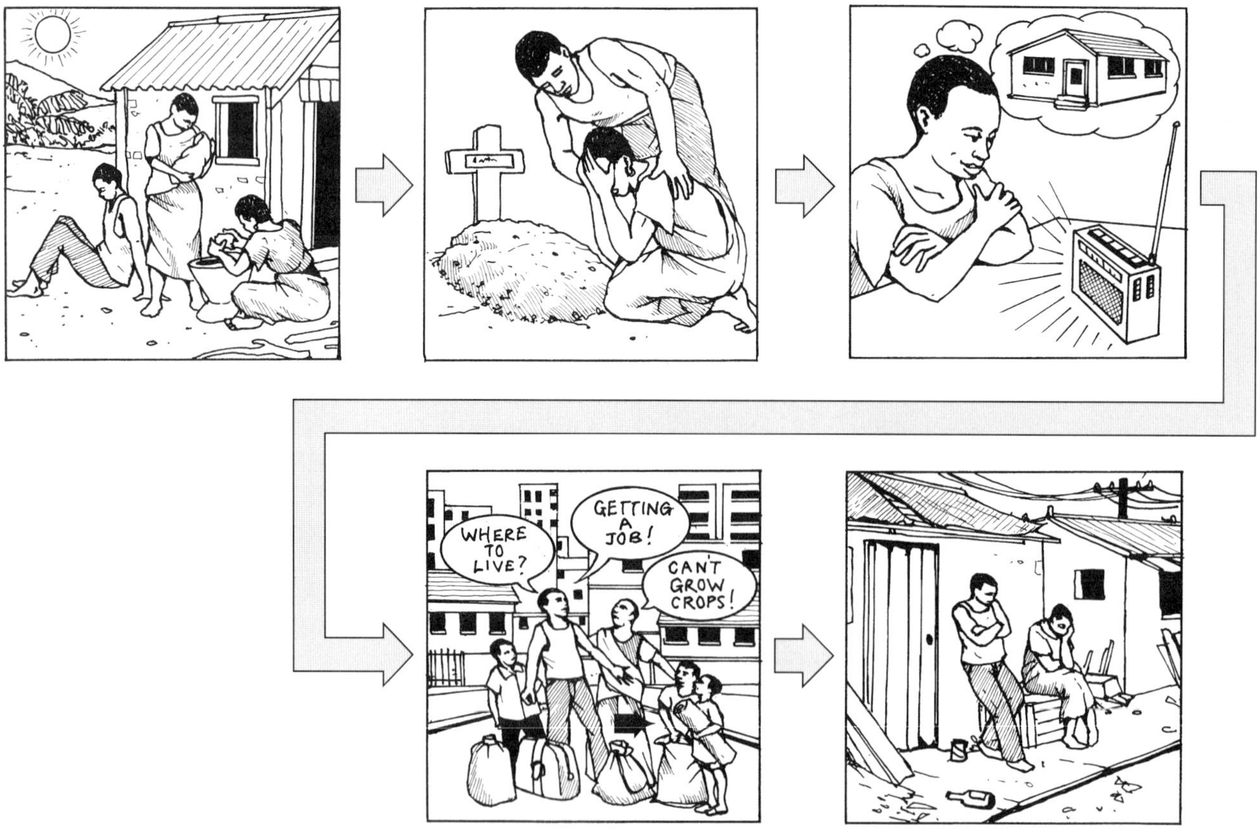
Arrival in the city. The problems we had …
Urban poverty. We now have …

You can recall this sequence of events with a list of letters, with each letter representing the information. Each letter is used to make up a saying to aid recall.

R	Rural poverty	Rude
Q	Quality of life	Questions
E	Expectations	Encourage
A	Arrival	Awful
U	Urban poverty	Uproar

Now try it for some of these topics:

- How people are affected by the closure of a coalmine. [📖 *164–165*]
- The provision of services in a rural area. [📖 *101*]
- Preparing for an earthquake. [📖 *14*]
- Coping with flooding in an LEDC. [📖 *37–39*]
- Effects of an oil spill on local communities. [📖 *200–201*]

2. GETTING ORGANISED

Key ideas

Key ideas help us organise our information about a **process**, a **cause and effect**, a **prediction** or a **geographical pattern**. These are the concepts which the key idea is developing. It's a generalised statement about a geographical feature. You have studied them by using real life examples or case studies. Examination questions are based on the key ideas. This means that each question will have a theme and one part leads on to the next.

A valuable revision task is to link the key ideas to the case study content. Understanding the key ideas helps you answer case study questions. If you download Specification A from the OCR website (www.ocr.org.uk), you will see the key ideas on pages 18, 20, 22, and 24 of the Specification. As you revise each part of the course, try to draw up a table like the one for Plate Tectonics below:

Key idea	What this means	Development
The distribution of earthquakes and volcanoes, related to plate margins	Where are plate margins, volcanoes and earthquakes found?	Maps of plates, volcanoes and earthquakes
The causes and effects of earthquakes and volcanic eruptions	Why do volcanoes erupt and earthquakes occur in particular places? What are volcanoes and earthquakes like?	How do people cope with danger? How do people make the most of opportunities created?
Why people live in areas of crustal instability	What are the advantages and disadvantages of living next to a volcano or in a place where earthquakes occur.	An example of how people cope with living near a volcano or in an earthquake area. You should be able to give different points of view

Case studies

Knowing facts and details is just the first stage. How to use this information in an examination is crucial. Many students begin revision by reading their notes. Just reading them through will not develop your understanding and could just create memory overload with a sense of not knowing anything!

To make the most of what you know, try to make links between the key idea and specific facts about places. This will create meaning from the information. Try using a template to summarise the main details of a case study. On the next page is an example for Tourism in Kenya. [📖 *158–159*]

Learning to Learn

Name of case study Kenya tourism	Location map 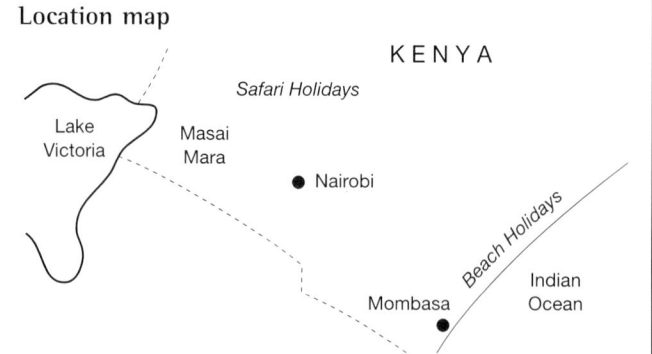
Key idea Tourism and its effects	
Key words Sustainability Trans National Companies (TNCs) Primary, secondary, tertiary Infrastructure	

Key questions
What are the benefits and problems caused by tourism for people, the environment and the economy?
Where do tourists come from?
What is the best way to manage tourism?

Benefits
Economic: provides jobs in services
develops infrastructure
investment by TNCs
local farmers and craft producers
can supply hotels/visitors

Environmental: pays for wildlife Game Parks

Social: increases visitors' awareness of LEDC

Problems
Social: clashes with traditional culture; traditional way of life becomes tourist attraction; encourages urban migration; crime increases

Economic: profits go abroad; jobs are seasonal, low paid and low skilled; many items imported; hotels owned by TNCs; tourism vulnerable to fuel price rises, wars etc.

Environmental: damage to game parks and coastal coral reefs, disruption to wildlife, soil erosion, too many vehicles, unsuitable buildings

Summary
Tourism is very important to Kenya but problems may outweigh advantages.
Control is by TNCs and depends on visitors from MEDCs.

Kenya would benefit more from tourism by:

- Having greater ownership of tourist schemes.
- Having more Kenyans involved in management.
- Protecting the Game Parks by limiting visitor numbers, zoning the parks to protect animals.
- Developing cultural centres for tourists to understand the Masai.
- Imposing quotas on imports to help local industry provide tourists' needs.
- Controlling the amount and style of tourist buildings.

The case study template must be adapted to suit the content and nature of the case study. Now try to produce a case study template for one of the following:

Causes and effects of a volcanic eruption [16–19]

Causes and effects of flooding in an LEDC [PRD 36–39]

The management of an eroding coast [48–51]

Characteristics of land use zones in urban areas [90–95]

Changes in rural areas [101–107]

Location of industry [152–155]

Consequences for communities as energy supplies change [164–165]

Causes and effects of acid rain [202–204]

Family planning policy [77]

Migration from one country to another [80–81]

Case study templates like these may be completed as part of a lesson. You could then put them together to produce a class revision booklet. Enlarged versions could be displayed in a 'case study corner'.

Your teacher will encourage you to use ICT to support your learning. Commercial CD ROMs can be used in revision alongside your own notes. Working together on the school network, it may be possible to create a Geography Intranet Revision Site.

Websites like BBC Bitesize (www.bbc.co.uk/schools/gcsebitesize/) include case studies which will widen your knowledge and understanding.

Key words

There are two groups of key words that are important: **specific geographical terms** and **the language of the examination**. Examination language includes command words [232–233].

In your geography lessons, you will have encountered terms which mean something specific in Geography. For example, 'power' means 'energy' in Geography but means 'influence' in History. For any key word you are unsure about, check it out in the glossary of a Geography book. [239] To help develop your geographical vocabulary, try these ideas:

In your notes, highlight important words and words which were new to you.

For each lesson, list the key words used.

Make your own glossary. Organise it by topic. This will help you link the words to the topic.

For each word, write a simple definition – one that you understand.

Make a wall display of key words for each topic.

3. THINKING THINGS THROUGH

Mind maps

Thinking things through will help develop your understanding. It is an important part of revision. See how a mind map develops. You can highlight different points using different colours. The mind map can be words or pictures. Figure 6 is part of a mind map, based on Tourism in Menorca. [156–157] It has three parts – the key idea, the links and questions, and case study details. Can you add to it?

The mind map allows you to write down what you know in any order. The questions help you to organise the detail and make links. Once you have drawn your mind map, you should be able to explain it to someone else. That should help you simplify it and focus on the essential detail.

FIGURE 6

Mind map

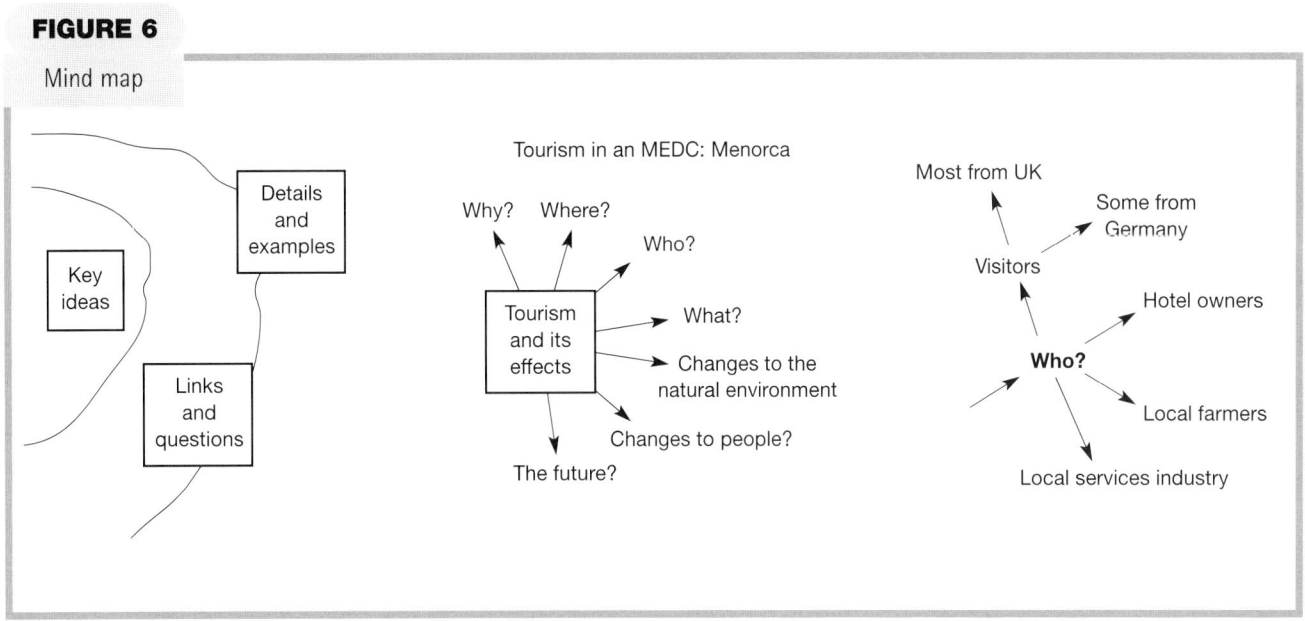

Learning to Learn

plate	earthquake	tsunami	subduction	Richter
tremor	plate margin	epicentre	fault	mantle
crust	trench	lava	oceanic ridge	volcano
ash cloud	fertile soil	geothermal	convergent	focus
magma	seismograph	time of day	buildings	prediction

Now try to develop mind maps for some of these:

Land use conflicts in National Parks [192–195]

Rapid industrial growth in a LEDC [136–138]

Factors affecting the density and distribution of population [68–69]

The characteristics of land use zones [90]

The causes, effects and management of river flooding [32 and 36]

Word games

Word games help you make links between unrelated words and ideas. They develop your ability to structure sentences in order to explain ideas. Start by listing 20 or 25 words from a topic. Above is an example from Plate Tectonics, done for you.

The word grid can be used to develop your understanding. Try these ideas:

Sort the words into groups. Think why you have grouped those words.

Choose four of the words carefully. Then ask a partner which word is the odd one out – and why.

Link five words from the grid into one sentence (that makes sense!)

Use the words as domino ends. For each domino, put two of the words onto an oblong card. The first player puts a card down; the next player adds a card if they can explain how their card links with the first card.

Memory maps and pictures

Try this in a group of three. Choose a map or diagram in a text book. Each person studies it for 30 seconds. Then together they redraw and annotate the map or diagram they studied. Set a time limit of three minutes, then compare the drawing with the original. In the same way, you can do this with annotated photographs. [145] You can spot the difference when you study two diagrams, maps or photographs showing change. [149] Go a stage further and try to predict future changes. For example, what will a scene look like in 100 years time where a coast is eroding [49] or where the development of tourism would change a view? [156].

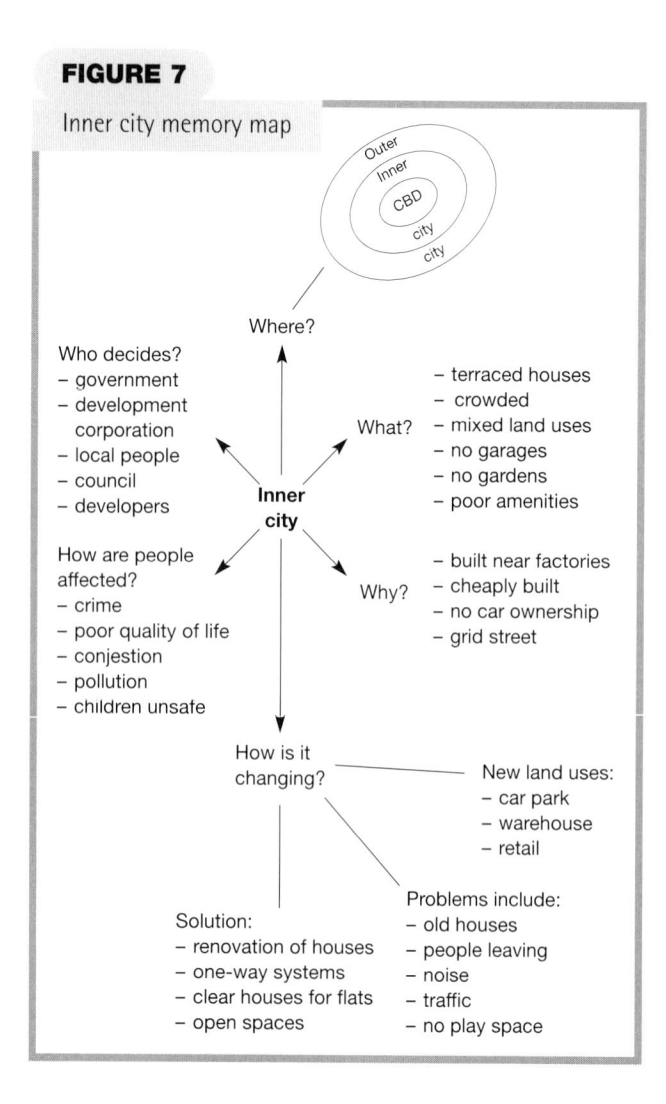

FIGURE 7

Inner city memory map

Where?
- Who decides?
  - government
  - development corporation
  - local people
  - council
  - developers

What?
- terraced houses
- crowded
- mixed land uses
- no garages
- no gardens
- poor amenities

Inner city

How are people affected?
- crime
- poor quality of life
- conjestion
- pollution
- children unsafe

Why?
- built near factories
- cheaply built
- no car ownership
- grid street

How is it changing?

Solution:
- renovation of houses
- one-way systems
- clear houses for flats
- open spaces

New land uses:
- car park
- warehouse
- retail

Problems include:
- old houses
- people leaving
- noise
- traffic
- no play space

Time lines and living graphs

These develop your understanding of the process of change. They help you place events in order and make links between them. Choose a suitable case study. From your notes, make a list of the facts, then draw a time line or graph and add the facts with arrows. Here's an example for a case study of a village affected by the closure of its coal mine. [📖 *164–165*]

Make a copy of the graph. Where on the graph would you add these?

- Coal mine closed.
- Holmewood rapidly grew.
- Miners leave the area.
- Enterprise zone opens.
- Increase in social problems.
- Many local shops close.
- 2299 mining jobs lost.
- Reclamation of spoil heaps.
- New housing built.

Now try this revision technique for some of these:

Changes in the rainforest caused by sustained forest clearance [📖 *184*]

Effects on tourism of a coastal oil spill [📖 *200–201*]

Effects of rising global temperature [📖 *207–208*]

Past papers

Past examination papers provide excellent revision material. They help put your other revision into a context. There is a lot to read on a question paper. By being familiar with the layout, instructions, language, the question structure and mark allocation, you will build your confidence. [📖 *62, 116, 170, 212*]

If you have a past paper:

Use a highlighter to pick out specific instructions on the cover.

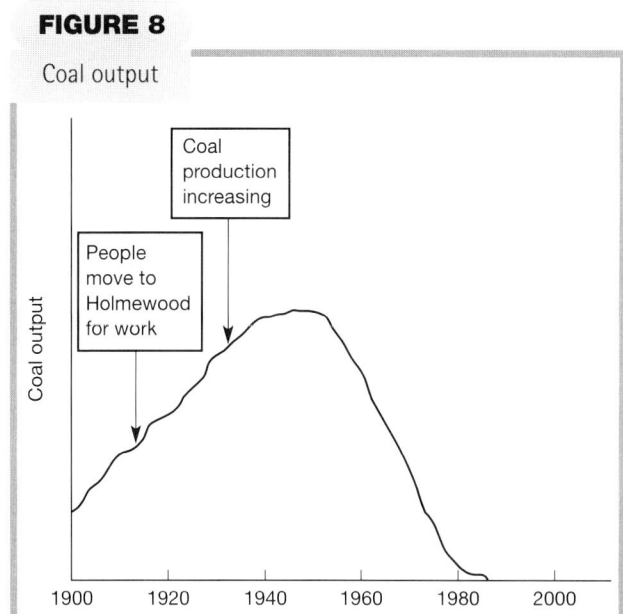

FIGURE 8

Coal output

Read the questions and write notes on the paper about what each question is about, what you have to do and how the marks are allocated.

Be clear how much you need to write. 1 mark means a short answer is expected, but 7 marks means you need to develop your ideas.

For each question, use a highlighter to pick out the command words.

Using another highlighter, pick out all the geographical terms. Check that you know their meaning before answering the question.

There is a time limit. Work out how many minutes to allow yourself for each question.

For questions which require a case study, decide which one you would use. Remember they are marked using levels. To gain high marks, your answer must be a detailed and place specific account.

After revising a topic for which you have a question on a past paper, set yourself a time limit to answer it. Your teacher may be able to provide a copy of the mark scheme so that you can see how well you did. Ask a friend to mark your answer, then discuss why your friend did not give you full marks!

People and the Physical World

The focus of this unit is the relationship between people and three aspects of the natural environment.

These are:
1. Plate Tectonics
2. Rivers
3. Coasts

Only the Rivers section is included in the Short Course specification.

PLATE TECTONICS

Plate tectonics is about the movement of the crustal plates and the earthquakes and volcanoes that are caused by this movement. [*6–23*]

You will need to revise

- a world map which shows the different types of plate margin.
- the different types of plate boundaries.

> **Memory maps/pictures**
> **Destructive/constructive margin diagrams**
>
> There are three diagrams of the different types of plate boundary [*PRD 8–9*]. You should be able to draw simple versions of these from memory and label them to show the processes which are occurring.
>
> Here are the labels to show what is happening at the destructive plate boundary – try to use them to produce a fully labelled diagram which you can learn to explain why volcanoes erupt at destructive plate margins.
>
> | Oceanic plate is more dense than continental plate | Magma builds up | Oceanic plate is subducted under continental plate |
> |---|---|---|
> | Crust is destroyed as a result of heat and pressure | Magma pushed through lines of weakness in crust | Plates move towards each other |
>
> Can you now produce similarly labelled diagrams for the constructive and transform plate boundaries too?

- where the main earthquake and volcano belts are located.
- what causes earthquakes and volcanoes to happen in certain areas of the world (these causes are often called 'tectonic processes').
- the effects which earthquakes and volcanic eruptions have.
- what people do in order to try to protect themselves from these effects.
- why many people still live in areas which may have earthquakes or volcanic eruptions.

> **Mnemonic**
>
> A good way to remember things is to learn a list of letters, with each letter representing the information.
>
> Learn the reasons why people live near volcanoes [*PRD 22-23*] by using WEARS (or perhaps SWEAR!)
>
> **W**arnings – *they believe they will be safe*
> **E**nergy – *hot rocks provide geothermal power*
> **A**ttracts tourists – *spectacular scenery*
> **R**esources – *volcanic rocks are rich in minerals*
> **S**oils – *many volcanic rocks produce fertile soil*

Make sure that you learn at least one case study of a volcano and one case study of an earthquake. Mount St Helens is a good example of a volcano. [*16–19*]

Remember: earthquakes and volcanoes are frequent events. Keep a file of any newspaper articles you read. There are also many websites that contain up-to-the-minute information about particular earthquakes or volcanic eruptions.

For each case study you will need to know:

- its location
- what caused it
- how it affected people and the environment
- how people have coped with the disaster
- what has been done since the disaster to make the area more prepared for another one

Remember: to score top marks for a case study answer you need to remember **details** of the particular location and event. You will see some examples of this later in the chapter.

RIVERS

The study can be divided into three main parts

1. The hydrological cycle
2. River processes and features
3. River flooding

The hydrological cycle is about how water moves around the environment. [*24–25*]

You will need to know:

- how this 'system' works with its inputs, flows, stores and outputs.
- the global system of water stores and transfers.
- river hydrographs which show a more localised system.
- how people can alter the river hydrograph.

Remember: as the name suggests a hydrograph is a graph! It is made up of a line graph and a bar graph. You may be asked to complete a graph or read data from it. You could also be asked questions about what pattern the graph shows.

FIGURE 9

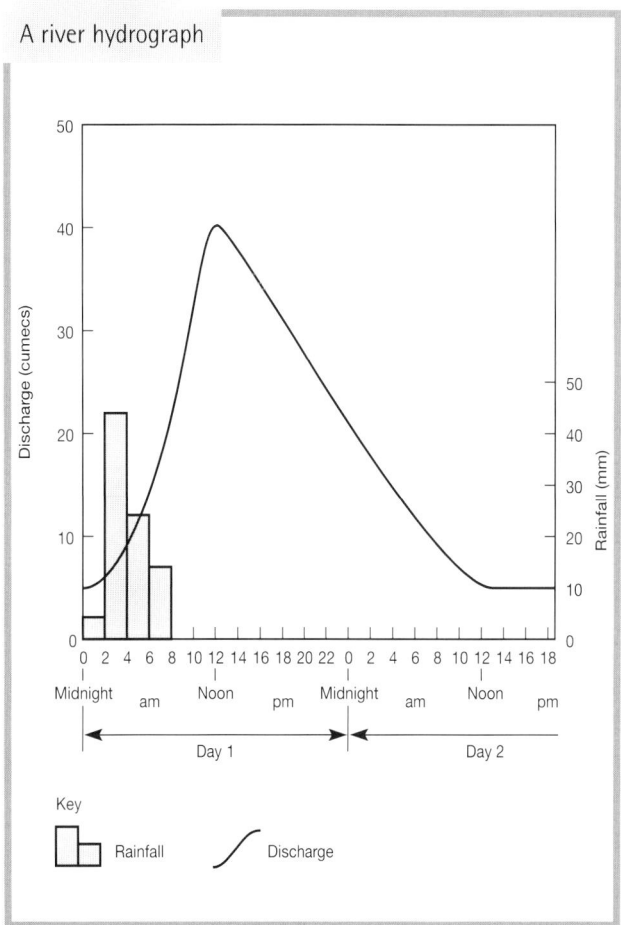

A river hydrograph

Time line/living graph
Hydrograph

Adding labels to graphs is a useful way of developing understanding. Figure 9 is a hydrograph to show how the discharge of a river changes after a period of heavy rain. You need to understand why the discharge changes so try to add these labels at the correct points on the graph. It should help you to learn both the processes involved and the geographical terminology to use.

Gentle falling limb

Steep rising limb

Overland flow reaches river quickly

Peak discharge

Short lag time

Groundwater maintains river flow at pre storm level

Water still reaching river from throughflow

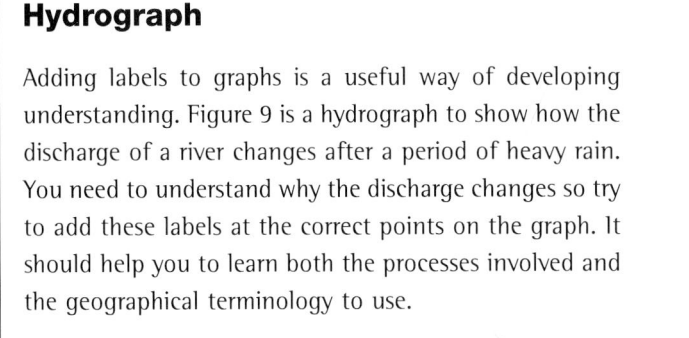

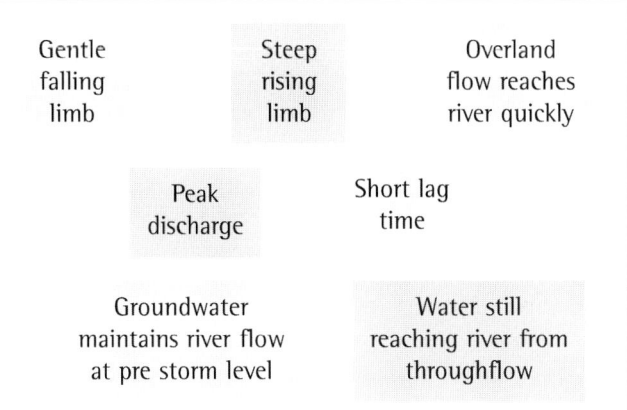

People and the Physical World

River processes are the ways that rivers change the landscape and create different features in the river valley. [26–31]

You will need to learn

- the four ways that a river can erode its bed and banks;
- the four ways that a river transports its load;
- why a river deposits its load;
- how a river produces different upper and lower course features such as waterfalls, interlocking spurs, meanders, ox bow lakes, levees and a flood plain.

Mnemonic

When you learn about the processes which shape a meander and sometimes create an ox bow lake, try learning DIB OBE:

Deposition	Outside
Inside	Bend
Bend	Erosion

Remember: you need to learn which features are formed by erosion and which are formed by deposition – and which are formed as a result of both processes.

Rivers overflow their banks and flood for many different reasons. The effects of flooding vary between countries depending on whether any defences have been created. [32–39]

You need to know

- what causes a river to flood;
- the effects of a river flood on the surrounding area;
- what people do to try to prevent a flood or how they deal with the consequences.

Mind maps Flooding

Mind maps help you to present a summary of what you know. Here an example has been started for you on the topic of flooding:

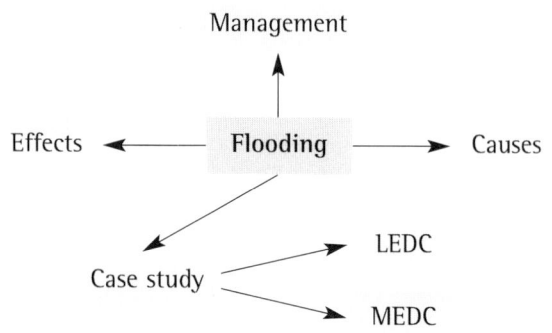

Use your notes and the textbook [32–39] to produce a mind map to help you learn this topic. You will need a large piece of paper so you can add details around each box.

Make sure you learn at least **two** case studies of river flooding, one must be from an MEDC (which could be UK or EU) and one example must be from an LEDC.

An example from an MEDC is the Netherlands. [32–35]

An example from an LEDC is Bangladesh. [36–39]

Remember: make sure that you know which case study is the MEDC and which is the LEDC. A question may only ask you about one!

A good way to organise your case study revision is to make a list of **all** your case studies and their locations. For each one, complete a template of important facts. You will see examples of these templates throughout the following chapters.

COASTS

The study can be divided into two parts:
1. processes and features;
2. what people do to protect sections of coastline vulnerable to erosion.

Some coastlines are permanently changed by the action of the sea. Like river flooding the effect of coastal change can depend upon the amount of protection that the coastline receives.

You will need to revise
- the ways that the sea erodes the coastline;
- how eroded material is transported by longshore drift;
- the features produced by erosion and deposition such as cliffs, headlands and bays, caves, arches, stacks and stumps, beaches, spits, bars and tombolos. [40–47]

💡 Coastal deposition features – sequence of formation

Sometimes learning how processes create landforms can be difficult. A sequence of diagrams may help. Draw the sequence to show how coastal features are formed by deposition. Learn the position of all the labels. It should help you to explain how spits, bars and tombolos are formed. After you have drawn it, try to add the labels in the correct places.

Remember: to help you to revise all the processes and features, make yourself a summary table or matrix such as the one shown below.

Erosion	Transport	Deposition
Processes	Description	Causes
Features		Features

You will also need to know:
- how the different erosion processes can alter or damage an area of coastline.
- what people do to try to protect the coastline or deal with the consequences of erosion.

💡 Word games: Coasts (odd one out)

On the topic of coasts, which words are the odd ones out in these two lists? Can you explain why?

If you work with a friend, you can write lists like this on any topic to test each other to make your revision more interesting.

List 1	List 2
CORRASION	REVETMENT
HYDRAULIC ACTION	TOMBOLO
SOLUTION	NATURAL ARCH
LONGSHORE DRIFT	SAND SPIT

You will need to learn at least one case study of how the sea is eroding part of the UK coastline and what is being done to protect or 'manage' this coastline.

Holderness, on the east coast of the UK is a good example of coastal management. [48–51]

💡 Fact or fiction – Case study Holderness

If you have studied Holderness, [48–51], work with a friend. You should each write 20 statements about Holderness on cards.

Some could be useful facts: e.g. the cliffs are easily worn away as they are made of boulder clay deposited during the Ice Age.

Others could be opinions: e.g. the money spent on protecting the coastline has been wasted.

Others could be inaccurate: e.g. Hornsea, Mappleton and Withernsea were villages which were washed into the sea.

Others could be irrelevant: e.g. global warming may result in a rise in sea level.

Once you have each written your sets of statements, you can swap the sets of cards and discuss where you do not agree with each other. Once you have both agreed on which are important facts you should make a list and learn them. It helps to produce revision cards which briefly list the main facts to learn – make sure some of them are place specific.

People and the Physical World

Remember: this case study can **only** be located in the UK. You may lose marks if you select an example from the wrong area. Your case study may be local to you if there is one that is appropriate. Your case study does not have to be a 'well known' example.

A DETAILED LOOK AT ONE QUESTION

Now that you know what you need to learn, have a look at the following question taken from a Higher Tier paper (Paper 2). Rather than trying to answer the question just yet, look at how a question can be divided into different parts. You will be able to see how the examiner has put the question together.

a) Study Fig. 10 below

FIGURE 10

Earthquake activity in northern Turkey 1939 to 1999

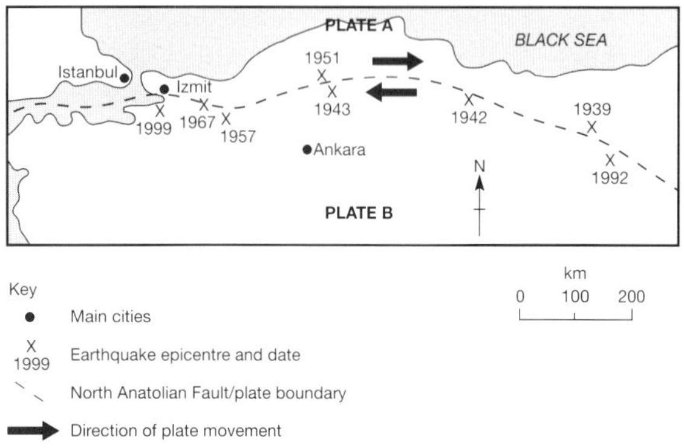

Key
- Main cities
- X 1999 Earthquake epicentre and date
- North Anatolian Fault/plate boundary
- Direction of plate movement

i) Measure the straight-line distance between the 1939 and 1999 earthquakes. [1]

ii) Describe the changing pattern of earthquake activity along the North Anatolian Fault between 1939 and 1999. [2]

iii) Explain why earthquake activity occurs along fault lines such as the North Anatolian Fault. [4]

b) Study Fig. 11 below.

FIGURE 11

Newspaper report following the earthquake in Turkey in 1999

UNSAFE BUILDINGS COST MANY LIVES.
Poorly built and maintained buildings were a significant factor in the huge death toll in Turkey's earthquake. Simple remedies could have strengthened many structures and made them 'earthquake proof'.

i) Suggest two ways in which buildings can be made earthquake proof. [2]

ii) What other actions can be taken so that people are well prepared for an earthquake? [3]

iii) Describe the effects of **either** the earthquake in Turkey **or** another earthquake in a named area which you have studied on people and the local economy. [7] [19]

The question is obviously about earthquakes, this is the **theme** of the question. [234–235]

Sections a(i) and a(ii) are testing **skills** to see if you can use the scale and can describe what is shown on the map.

Remember: not all 'skills' questions are on Papers 3 and 4. There are always some marks that test geographical skills on Papers 1 and 2.

Remember: to read carefully the **command words** which are used throughout the question. [232–233]

It is very important to know what these command words mean. Don't lose marks by explaining when you should be describing, for instance. You will not score full marks if you get them mixed up.

In part a(iii), you need to use your understanding of what causes earthquakes to explain why they happen along the fault line. Use the clue from the map, which shows that the two plates, either side of the fault line, are moving in opposite directions.

Section b continues the theme of earthquakes but now focuses on how people try to protect themselves. If you use your knowledge of making buildings 'earthquake-proof' and of other protection measures you can suggest what people may be able to do in Turkey. Examiners call this use of your knowledge '**application**'. In other words, you are using what you have learned in a new situation. So you do not need to have studied 'earthquakes in Turkey' to answer this question.

The final section of this question is the case study. This is a very important part of the answer and usually accounts for the highest number of marks in a section.

> **Remember:** a good case study answer needs detailed knowledge of the topic.

It is important that you can write about the effects of one particular earthquake rather than earthquakes in general.

Examiners mark all case studies in the same way. The system is called '**levels marking**'. To score the highest level, it is necessary to include detailed and specific information which you have learned. Examples of the use of a levels mark scheme are given later in the chapter.

FIGURE 12

Landforms along a stretch of coastline

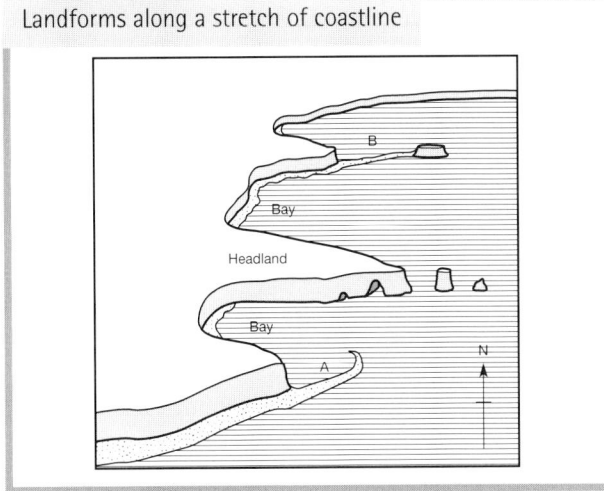

Tasks to do

Study this question which is taken from a Higher Tier examination paper.

Then:

- Identify the question theme.
- Pick out the command words in each section.
- Decide a suitable case study to use.

a) Study Fig. 12.

  i) Identify the coastal landforms at A and B. [2]

  ii) Suggest reasons why there are bays and headlands along this stretch of coastline. [2]

  iii) Name the main features which have formed on the headland. Explain, by referring to coastal processes, how these features have been formed. You may draw fully labelled diagrams as part of your answer. [7]

b) Study Figs. 13a and 13b.

FIGURE 13a

Slapton Sands and Start Bay

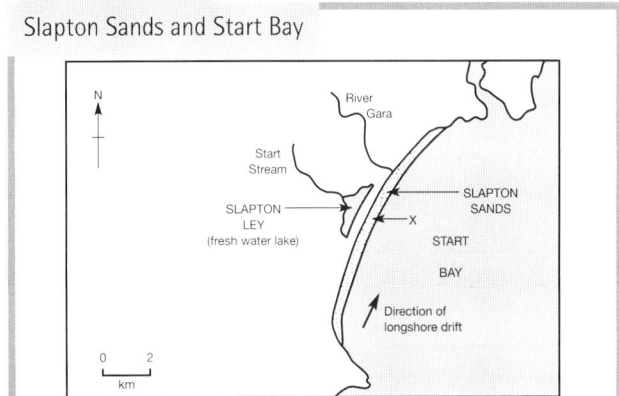

FIGURE 13b

A student's field sketch of Slapton Sands

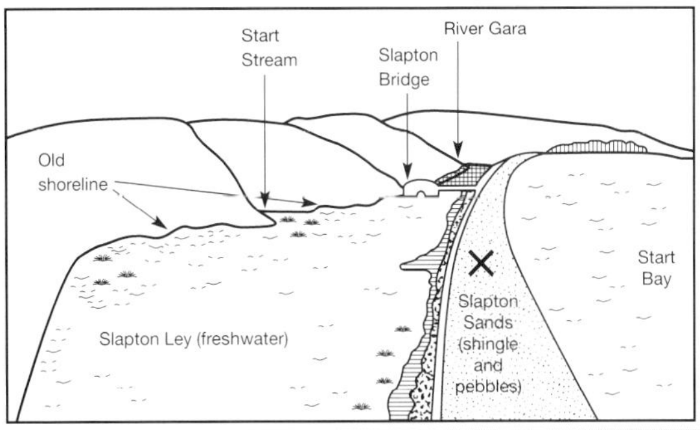

  i) Slapton Sands is a bar. Briefly describe, using evidence from Figs. 13a and 13b only, the main features of Slapton Sands. [3]

  ii) Describe the processes which have shaped this stretch of coastline. [5] [19]

People and the Physical World

CASE STUDY ANSWERS

All questions in Papers 1 and 2 contain a case study which will test your knowledge of a real place example. Case studies are worth most marks in each question and therefore it is vital that you are able to produce high scoring answers. The following question focuses on a case study of an earthquake.

> Describe the effects of an earthquake in a named area, which you have studied, on people and the economy.

A good technique for revising case studies is to create a **template** or framework to show what you have learned. It is particularly useful to complete a template as you are revising each case study.

Below is an example of a template for this question.

Remember: choose a question from a previous year's exam paper and fill in sections like these, using your notes.

Creating a template will help you to focus on what knowledge is needed and help you to remember the details.

Tasks to do

Use your notes and look at these websites below to draw and complete case study templates for the following questions:

> http://www.geoexplorer.co.uk/sections/links/tectonicactivity.htm
>
> http://www.georesources.co.uk/tectonicg.htm
>
> http://www.quake.seismo.unr.edu/ftp/pub/louie/class/100/plate-tectonics.html
>
> http://www.volcano.und.nodak.edu
>
> http://www.aist.go.jp/GSJ/~jdehn/v-home.htm

Name of case study – include location: Kobe in Japan	

Key idea:
How an earthquake in Japan affected the area of Kobe
	Key words:
	  effects
	  immediate or short-term
	  long-term
	  casualties
	  buildings
	  transport
	  industry
	  economy

Do not write about: The causes of the earthquake	
Ideas to include with details:	
People	Economy
How many died?	Which buildings collapsed and where?
How many were injured?	How were transport communications disrupted?
What caused outbreak of disease?	Why could people not go to work?
Why were many people homeless?	What infrastructure was destroyed and how?
What were there shortages of?	What were the costs of re-building?
What were people afraid of?	Why did it have long-term effects on the economy?

- For a named volcano which you have studied explain the causes of the volcanic eruption and how it affected the surrounding area.

Name and location of case study:	
Key idea:	Key words:
Do not write about:	
Ideas to include with details:	
Causes	Effects

- Describe the methods which have been used to protect the coastline from erosion in a named area which you have studied.

The examiner will mark your case study answer using 'levels'. This means that you will get more marks for a detailed answer than one which is vague and could really be about anywhere.

Remember: the secret of a good case study answer is to include some real 'place knowledge' in your answer.

This is how the case study is marked

A typical mark scheme for the earthquake case study question is as follows:

Level 1: (low marks)
The candidate's answer includes statements with limited detail which describe the effects of an earthquake.

Level 2: (medium marks)
The candidate's answer includes more developed statements which describe the effects of an earthquake.

Level 3: (high marks)
The candidate's answer includes comprehensive and place-specific statements which describe the effects of an earthquake.

By itself this is not very helpful for the candidate or the examiner. However, the following example, for Kobe, will show the types of statements that fit into each level.

Level 1:
- Lots of people were killed and injured.
- Many houses collapsed.
- Roads were blocked by falling buildings.
- It left people homeless.
- Lots of fires broke out across the city.

Level 2:
- Nearly 5000 people died.
- Over 14,000 people were injured.
- Most people died through being crushed by collapsed houses.
- Electricity supplies were cut off across the city as cables were cut.
- Many of the large factories in the industrial district were badly damaged and so production had to stop.

Level 3
- Large areas of the central city were set alight by fires starting from broken gas pipes which made it impossible for the rescue services to enter the city centre.
- The Hanshin Expressway, a main route through Kobe, collapsed on the road below. This occurred where the road crossed areas of softer, wetter ground where the shaking was stronger and lasted longer.
- The port area was particularly badly affected as it had been constructed on two artificial islands, which suffered from liquefaction. The port had to be closed for two months, which meant that trade had to be switched to other ports.
- The economic effects of the earthquake were widespread. There was a drop in the production of steel. Car plants throughout Japan had to close or cut production, as there was a shortage of parts which were made in Kobe.

Tasks to do

Over the page are the case study answers of three candidates. You must decide which answers are Levels 1, 2 and 3. What is the evidence on which you have made your decision?

People and the Physical World

Answer 1

The earthquake in Taiwan on 21 September 1999 affected many people. The focus of the earthquake was near the surface and the focus was near Puli, a major city. Therefore many businesses were disrupted. Many people were trapped in the rubble of their houses as the earthquake of magnitude 7.6 occurred during the early hours of the morning. Production rates fell as factories were closed forcing a fall in the economy. Many people died and those who survived had to live with no water, electricity or telecommunications. Main highways and bridges were destroyed so there was no way into the city apart from helicopter which is how medical supplies and food aid entered. Taiwan is a NIC and so has a fragile economy which would have been greatly hit.

Answer 2

The effects of the earthquake in San Francisco (on the San Andreas fault line) were dreadful. The city was overcrowded and to make way for all the people, roads had been built on top of each other and houses were built closer to the fault line. When the earthquake happened the effects were disastrous, people did not expect an earthquake of this size and so were unprepared. Roads collapsed, buildings crumbled and houses were reduced to rubble. Even though a million dollars worth of damage was caused, the death toll was low. If such an earthquake had occurred in an LEDC there would have been more deaths because of the lack of basic emergency services.

Answer 3

Recent earthquakes in San Francisco, California, have resulted in many people losing their homes. This is because a large area of housing is built on reclaimed land. When an earthquake occurs, its destructive power is multiplied because of liquefaction. Many homes in the Marina district of the city were built on soft wet land and waves in the earth caused a lot of buildings to collapse. Many people were left homeless and water had to be brought in by tanker because the drinking water was infected. A road bridge across the bay, which had two layers of traffic on it, collapsed in on itself. The baseball stadium had to be evacuated as large cracks began to appear in the walls and terraces. Billions of dollars worth of damage was caused. People could not go to work because the roads were blocked or the factories and offices were unsafe, so millions of dollars were lost from the economy.

Tasks to do

There are some examples of case study answers below. They are all answers to the same question. After each example, there is a task for you to do about each answer. Rather than writing your answer, you may wish to discuss it with a partner.

For a named river which has flooded, explain why it flooded and the effects of the flood.

Answer 1 (from Paper 1)

The River **Tyne** flooded because the streams that ran into it were fast flowing, plus heavy rainfall caused the banks to burst. The flooding caused crops to be ruined and damage to homes.

Why was this answer only marked as a Level 1 answer?

Answer 2 (from Paper 1)

The **Trent** flooded near Nottingham because there was very heavy rain for three months. A lot of the land near the river has been used for building new houses and so the water quickly ran into the river so that the level rose above the river banks.

No one was killed by the floods but the homes of many people were affected by the floodwater which caused thousands of pounds worth of damage. People had to be moved out of their homes as the floodwater rose. Many farmers lost their crops which were ruined by the water. Many roads were shut so that people could not get to work.

What are the good points of this answer? How could it be improved to make it a Level 3 answer?

Answer 3 (from Paper 2)

The River **Brahmaputra** in Bangladesh floods regularly. The main reason for this is that in Nepal, a nearby country in the Himalayas, they have cut down huge forests. These are cut down and burned as fuel wood. This then makes the soil vulnerable and it is eroded. Every year when the monsoon comes,

Bangladesh receives heavy rainfall and also all the rain that fell in Nepal flows down the river. This is because there are no trees to stop the rain and the soil is so thin so it does not absorb it. The water runs down the steep slopes and into the river causing it to flood.

The effects are disastrous. The crops are destroyed from the rain resulting in starvation in most of the country. Animals are drowned as the water level rises or as there is no food for them. Whole villages are destroyed as the type of housing is of low standard, usually made from mud or clay which disintegrates leaving many homeless. Services find it hard to cope as main routes become blocked. Everyone goes into a state of panic. Over half of Bangladesh is below sea level so most of the country is flooded. Places of work are destroyed so people are unable to work.

Which is the weak part of this answer – the causes or the effects? How could it be improved?

Answer 4 (from Paper 2)

In 1993 the River **Mississippi** flooded because of a number of reasons. Very heavy rain in Spring and melting snow meant that the land became saturated and drains could not cope. Thunderstorms in June resulted in rapid runoff. Further storms in July put pressure on the levees which eventually collapsed. Building new urban areas on the flood plain resulted in increased runoff due to the land being impermeable.

The flood plain was covered by metres of water and an area bigger than Britain was affected by flooding. All road and railway bridges south of St Louis were damaged or destroyed. River traffic was stopped for several months as the current was too strong. The floods caused 43 deaths and 50,000 were evacuated from their homes. $8billion of damage was caused. The water stayed on the land for several months, this water became stagnant and attracted rats and mosquitoes. Sewage was washed into the river which led to outbreaks of disease like dysentery. Millions of dollars have been spent on new flood defences to try to stop it from happening again.

This is a good case study. Explain why it is a Level 3 answer.

Tasks to do

Severe floods which occurred in Central and Eastern Europe in August 2002. They were used by two candidates to answer this question.

Explain the causes and describe the effects of a river flood in an MEDC which you have studied.

Here are their answers. They have tried to use the information which they have learned from this case study.

Look at this list of eight characteristics of case study answers. Decide which four apply to the answer given by Candidate 1 and which four to Candidate 2.

A Uses geographical terminology.
B Makes simple statements.
C Includes information which is not relevant.
D Develops (expands) on points which are made.
E Does little to explain the causes of the floods.
F Includes relevant facts and figures.
G Gives a place-specific answer (writes about the actual places).
H Makes inaccurate, sweeping statements.

Candidate 1's answer

The rivers in Germany flooded in August 2002 when it rained in August 2002. Lots of people were drowned when all the rivers burst their banks. All the houses and cars were washed away and floods caused pollution in Germany. The Austrian government had to pay for the damage and had to cut its order for Eurofighter jets from 24 to 18.

Candidate 2's answer

After heavy rain in August 2002 the River Elbe in Germany flooded. The high water levels were the result of rain falling for several days which saturated the soil and caused river levels to rise rapidly. The building of homes and factories within the area made the floods worse as runoff was more rapid from the impermeable surfaces. Houses and factories which had been built on the flood plains were damaged. In historic cities, such as Dresden, historical buildings such as museums and churches were damaged along with their valuable contents. Bridges, railway lines and roads were also damaged therefore transport was disrupted and people could not get to work. The German railways lost 7 million euros and the total loss is estimated at 15–20 billion euros. The environment was also affected as the rivers were polluted by toxins which were washed into the river.

Answers:

Candidate 1:   B, C, E, H
Candidate 2:   A, D, F, G

two
People and Places to Live

This unit is divided into two sections:

- Population.
- Settlement.

Only the Settlement section is included in the Short Course Specification

POPULATION

The **population** section can be divided into three different parts:

Density and distribution of population

1. 'Density and distribution of population' is about where people live. [📖 *68–71*] You will need to revise:

   - the difference between density and distribution of population;
   - what causes a high population density in some areas and a low population density in other areas.

   You will need to know **two** case studies, one to explain the reasons for a high population density in an area and another to explain the reasons for a low population density.

   For each case study you must learn:

   a) the name of your case study area and its location;

   b) the reasons why many (or few) people live there.

   Remember: you will only score high marks for your case study answer if you know **details** about your named area.

   There are many reasons to explain population density. They can be divided into three main groups:

   - Physical reasons: climate, relief of the land, soil fertility, natural vegetation.
   - Economic reasons: raw material exploitation, transport systems, employment opportunities.
   - Social reasons: standard of living, services available, people for support.

Population structure

   Remember: a good way to remember all the details is to summarise them in three star diagrams: Physical reasons, Economic reasons, Social reasons.

2. 'Population structure' is about the gender and age balance of a population and usually refers to a whole country. You are most likely to study population structure through a population pyramid. [📖 *72–73*] You will need to revise:

   - how to complete and understand a population pyramid graph;
   - what the term, 'population structure' means and why it varies between countries;
   - how the population structure of a country affects decisions which are made about the future.

   You will need to know in detail the population structure of one LEDC **and** one MEDC (this may be the UK).

Population change

3. 'Population change' is about how the number of people living in an area changes over time. [📖 *74–75*] You will need to revise:

   - why birth rates and death rates vary between different countries;
   - how birth rates and death rates change over time;
   - how birth rates and death rates affect population structure.

FIGURE 14

Time line/living graph

Stage 1
Stage 2
Stage 3
Stage 4
Birth rate & death rate per 1,000
Birth rate
Natural increase – the difference between the birth rate and death rate
Death rate
Time

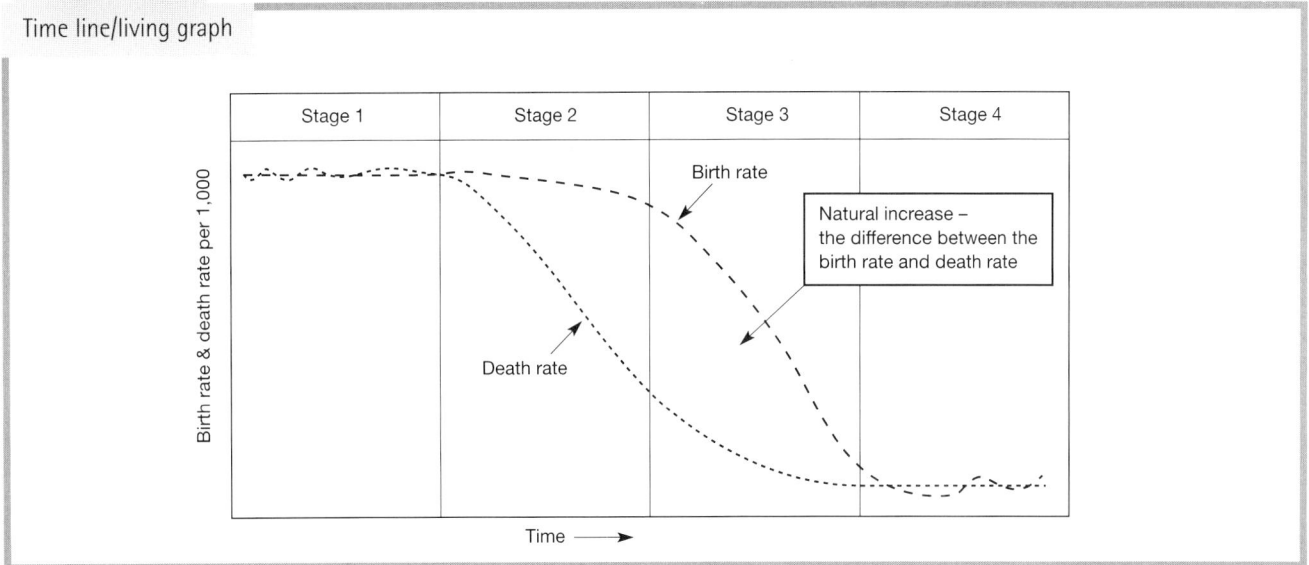

Your case study is one country where population numbers are changing due to different reasons. A popular example is China (77) but there are lots of other examples.

FIGURE 15

Population structure of a country

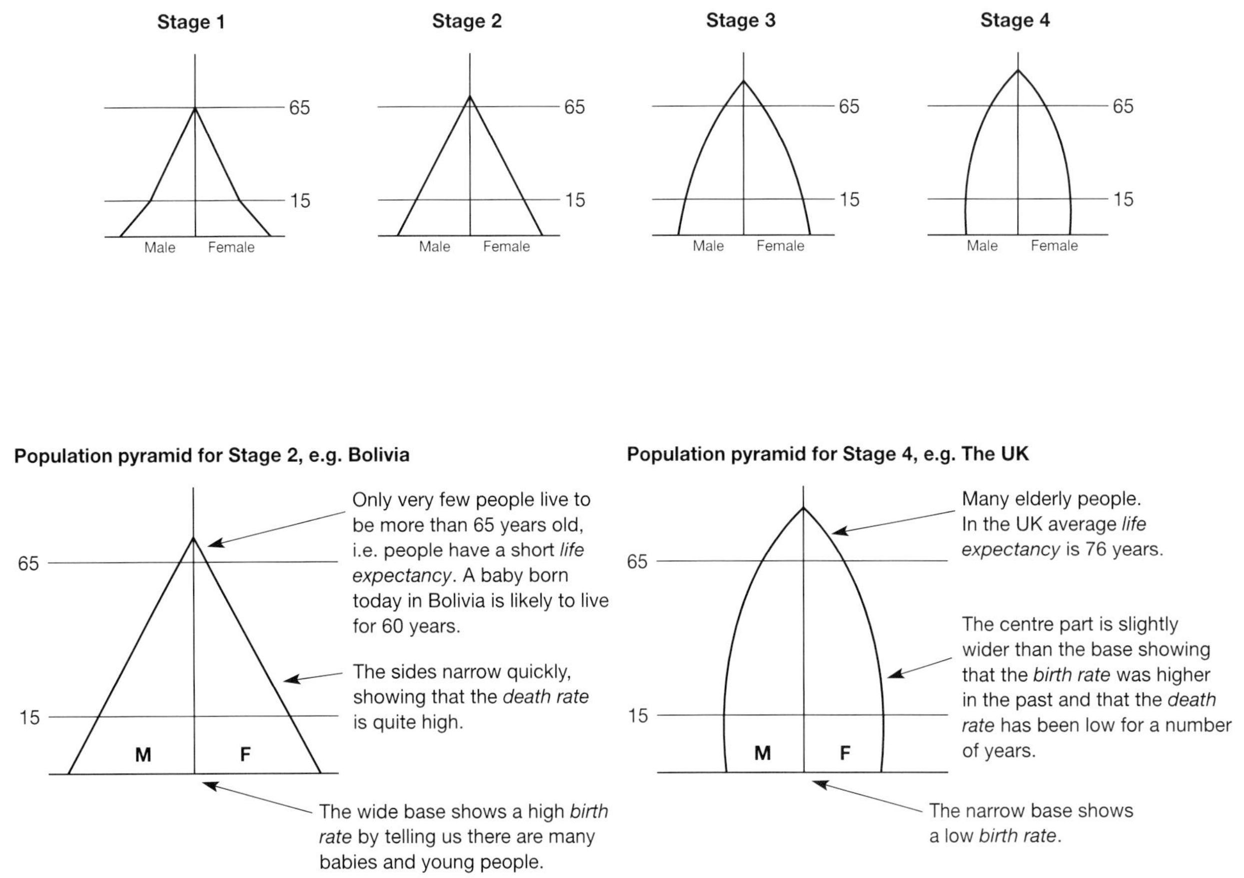

Stage 1
Stage 2
Stage 3
Stage 4
65
15
Male
Female
Population pyramid for Stage 2, e.g. Bolivia
Only very few people live to be more than 65 years old, i.e. people have a short *life expectancy*. A baby born today in Bolivia is likely to live for 60 years.
The sides narrow quickly, showing that the *death rate* is quite high.
The wide base shows a high *birth rate* by telling us there are many babies and young people.
M
F
Population pyramid for Stage 4, e.g. The UK
Many elderly people. In the UK average *life expectancy* is 76 years.
The centre part is slightly wider than the base showing that the *birth rate* was higher in the past and that the *death rate* has been low for a number of years.
The narrow base shows a low *birth rate*.

People and places to live

You also need to revise:

- why many people move from one country to another – these are usually called 'push' and 'pull' factors.

You will need to learn a case study of international migration (from one country to another). You should explain why lots of people have moved and how their migration affects the two countries. [📖 80–81]

Fact or fiction – a case study of international migration

You should work with a friend and use the case study of migration from Mexico to the USA [📖 80–81] to write 20 statements each on cards.

Some could be useful facts: e.g. Mexicans migrate to the USA as they are attracted by pull factors such as the wealth and 'bright lights' image.

Others could be opinions: e.g. The Americans should prevent Mexicans migrating to the USA by employing more border patrols.

Other could be inaccurate: e.g. Only the poorest Mexicans migrate to the USA, few of them have any skills.

Others could be true but irrelevant: e.g. It will take 116 years for the population of the USA to double.

Swap your set of statements and see if your partner agrees with those which you think are important facts, then make a list of those and learn them. Make sure some of the facts are **developed** and **place specific**. E.g. many Mexicans migrate *to the Central Valley of California* (place specific point) to get jobs *picking fruit and vegetables or they work in food processing factories* (developed point).

You also need to know:

- how this migration affects the rural area which they leave.
- why people settle in squatter settlements (shanty towns) in the cities that they migrate to.
- what problems people have in squatter settlements and what is done to improve them.

Your case study must be from an LEDC. There are lots of examples of rural to urban migration. Two popular case studies focus on movement in Bangladesh [📖 84–89] and Brazil. Now look at the Memory Picture (Figure 16).

Mnemonic – rural to urban migration in LEDCs

Use this list of letters to learn the 'push' factors which encourage people to migrate from rural areas in LEDCs.

Soil erosion
Insufficient health care
Drought
Overgrazing
Famine
Reform of land
Unemployment
Mechanisation

Remember 'Sid of Rum'. Now can you work out a list of letters to help you learn the 'pull' factors?

Remember: do not get mixed up between international migration (from one country to another) and rural to urban migration (within an LEDC).

SETTLEMENT

The **settlement** section is divided into five parts:

Rural to urban migration

1. 'Rural to urban migration' is about the movement of people from the countryside to towns and cities. [📖 84–89] You will need to know the following:

   - the reasons why people move or migrate.

Land use zones in urban areas

2. 'Land use zones in urban areas' is about the different parts of a city. [📖 90–95] You will need to know about the following areas:
   - CBD.
   - inner zone or inner suburbs.
   - outer suburbs.
   - rural–urban fringe.

This case study must be a town or city in the UK. [📖 91–95]

Mind maps – Urban Land Use zones

A mind map has been started here to help you to present a summary of what you know about urban land use. Use your notes and your textbook [📖 90–99] to produce a mind map to help you learn this topic. Make sure that you add details around each box to help you to learn the topic.

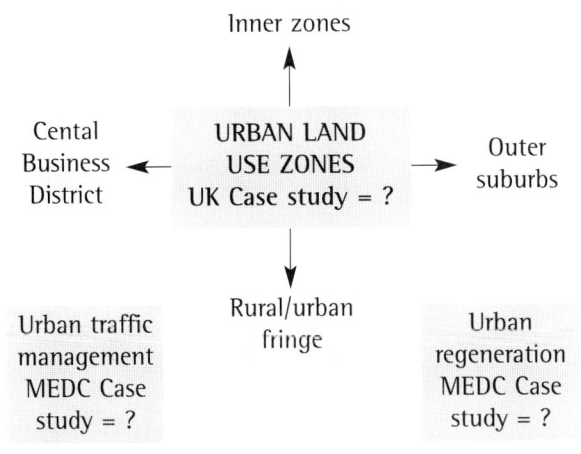

Ways to improve quality of life in cities

3. Ways to improve quality of life in cities is about how planning changes make areas better for people who live there. [📖 96–99] You need to learn at least **two** case studies:

- traffic management in a city.
- urban regeneration which means renewing an area of a city.

For this second topic you may have studied an old inner city area or a former docklands, such as Swansea.

Remember: these case studies do not have to be from the UK. They can be in any MEDC, including EU countries.

FIGURE 16
Memory picture of rural to urban migration

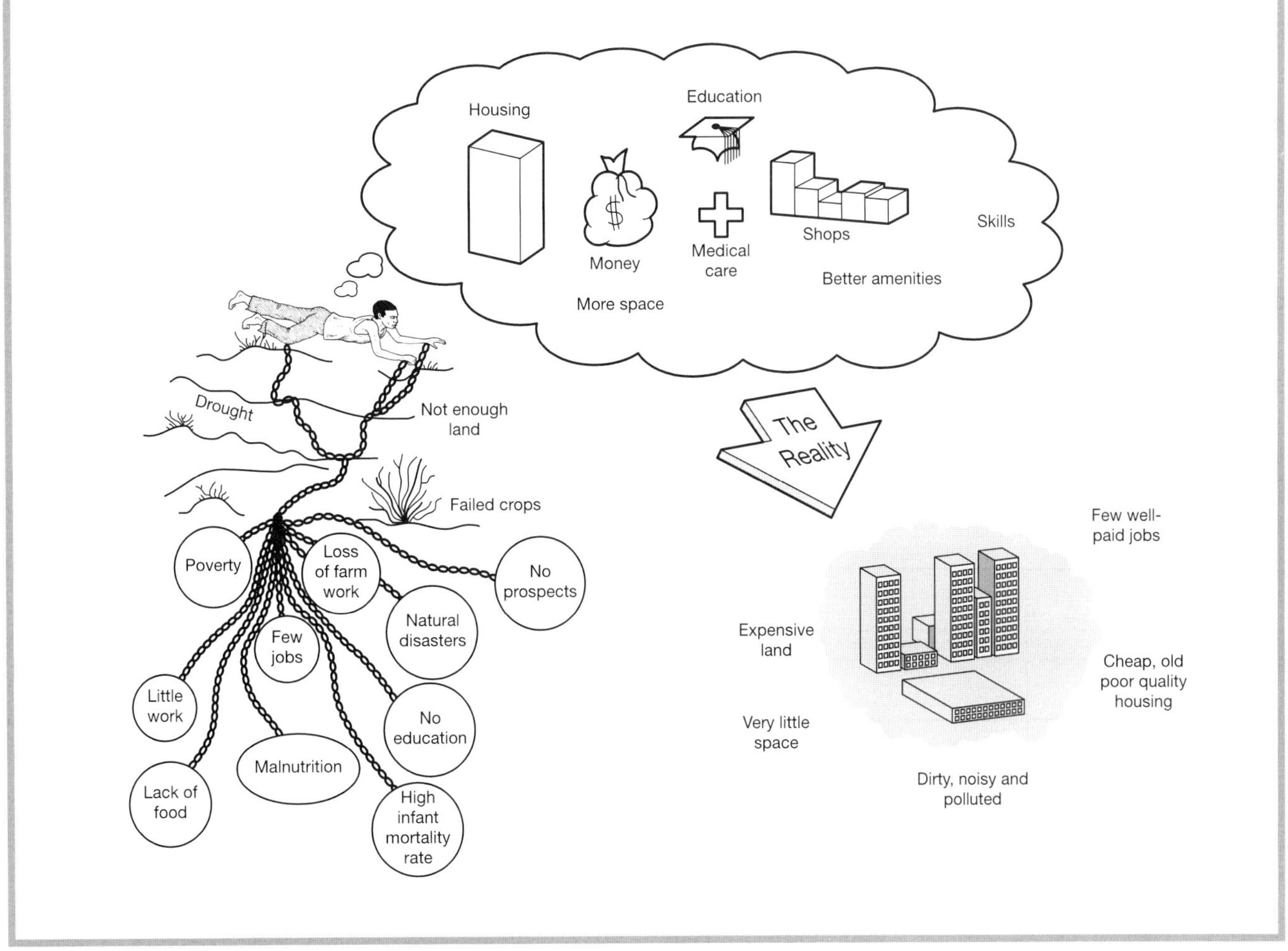

People and places to live

Providing services in rural and urban areas

4. 'Providing services in rural and urban areas' is about where people do their shopping or have access to services such as transport. Services will only be available if there are enough people to make them worthwhile or profitable, so only a few services will be found in all settlements and some services will only be available in cities.

Remember: 'rural' refers to the countryside and 'urban' refers to towns and cities.

You need to know:

- what 'service hierarchy' means.
- examples of different settlements in a hierarchy.
- what are 'high' and 'low' order services and to give some examples.

Remember: to help you to revise the relationships between settlements and services, make a summary matrix such as the one below and put in your own hierarchy.

You need to learn the details of the hierarchy in one area of any MEDC, including the UK. [102–104]

Newer shopping centres are sometimes located on the edge of urban areas, near to motorways. Learn:

- the features of out of town shopping centres, such as Blue Water near London, Meadowhall near Sheffield, MetroCentre near Newcastle.
- Why they were built at these locations and how they affect the surrounding areas.

How rural areas are changing where people move into them

5. 'How rural areas are changing where people move into them'. [105–107] You will need to know:

- why people are moving from towns and cities (urban areas) to the countryside (rural areas).

Remember: do not get mixed up between rural to urban migration in LEDCs and urban to rural migration in the UK.

- the effects on villages of many new residents moving in.
- what people in the villages (both original and new residents) think about these changes.

Remember: 'what people think' is often referred to as 'attitudes and values' in the question paper.

Know the details of urban to rural migration in one area of the UK, such as North Worcestershire.

	Settlement	Example	Service	
Largest	City	Newcastle	Airport	High order
	Town	Whitley Bay	Library	
	Village	Horsley	General store	
Smallest	Hamlet	Milbourne	Post box	Low order

A New Introduction to Geography for OCR GCSE Specification A: Revision Guide

Word games – Settlement

Here are 25 words or phrases on the topic of settlement.

urban	park and ride	hierarchy
commute	neighbourhood centre	suburbs
inner city		gentrification
sphere of influence	by-pass	detached housing
	rural	
counter urbanisation	planners	green belt
	high order services	pedestrianised
regeneration		terraced housing
congestion	sustainable	
accessible	out of town shopping centre	
quality of life		

Make sentences using the words in the grid to help you learn your case studies. Try to use as many of these words as you can in each sentence. Here is an example.

Gentrification has occurred in the Sharrow area of inner city Sheffield as the quality of life has been improved in areas of terraced housing.

DIFFERENT TYPES OF QUESTIONS

The examination papers contain different types of question that aim to test what you have learned. They are testing your

- knowledge – what facts and details you have learned;
- understanding – what you can work out;
- application – how you can transfer your understanding to another place or situation;
- skills – whether you can draw or interpret maps, graphs etc.

It helps if you are able to recognise the different types of question because it will guide your answer in the right direction as the following example answers show.

All examination questions at both Foundation and Higher tier contain a variety of these types – and some questions may link two types together.

Here are two examination questions that show how the different types of question are used. Some parts are from Foundation Tier and some from Higher Tier.

Question 1

(a) Many farming villages which are located near big cities in the UK have changed into villages where commuters live. **What is a commuter?** *Knowledge*

(b) i) Use the following information to **complete the graph**. *Skills*

   ii) **Suggest two reasons** why the population of such villages has increased since 1951. *Understanding*

(c) **Identify two changes** to the bus timetable between 1970 and 2000. *Skills*

(d) Study the signs on two houses in the village.

   i) **What do the two signs suggest** about the village? *Application*

   ii) **How could the changes** shown on the house signs **affect** people who live in the village? *Knowledge and Understanding*

(e) i) Many new shopping centres are located away from town and city centres. **Give two reasons** why. *Understanding*

   ii) Refer to a new shopping centre which is located away from a town or city centre.

   Name the shopping centre and **describe** its effects on the town or city centre and the area surrounding the new shopping centre. *Knowledge*

Question 2

(a) i) **From the population pyramid** of Ethiopia, **identify** the age group which contains the largest percentage of both males and females. *Skills*

   ii) **Define** the term 'dependant population'. **How does** the dependant population **shown in the population pyramids** differ between Ethiopia and the Netherlands? *Knowledge and Skills*

   iii) **How** do differences in birth rate and life expectancy affect the shapes of the two population pyramids? *Application*

(b) **With reference to one named country** which you have studied **describe** attempts to control the birth rate. *Knowledge*

(c) Study the Government report on UK population.

   i) **Suggest two reasons** for the ageing trend of the population in the UK. *Understanding*

   ii) **What** will be the consequences of an ageing population? *Knowledge and Understanding*

People and places to live

Tasks to do

Now it's your turn to think about what type of question you are being asked. Don't try to answer the question. (You can't because you don't have the resources!) Just decide whether the questions are testing knowledge, understanding, application or skills, or a combination of two of them.

Question 3 (from a Foundation paper)

(a) Study the bar graphs.

   i) **What percentage** of the residents of Ashley are unemployed?

   ii) **Complete the graph** by drawing a bar to show the following information:

   iii) **Use the graph to complete** the table below which ranks the percentage of owner occupied houses in the five parts of Bristol.

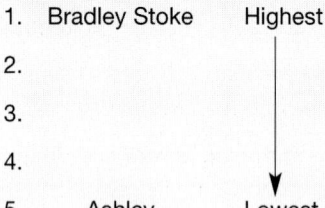

   1. Bradley Stoke   Highest
   2.
   3.
   4.
   5. Ashley   Lowest

   iv) Bradley Stoke is an area on the edge of Bristol. **Suggest why** only 5% of households do not have a car

   over 30% of the population moved into the area last year

   over 90% of the houses are owner occupied

(b) Study the street map of part of the inner city area of Bristol.

   Describe four possible problems for people who live in areas like that shown.

(c) In parts of many towns and cities planners have tried to improve the quality of life through developments such as regeneration schemes and urban traffic management.

   For a town or city which you have studied in the UK or EU, **describe** how this has been done.

(d) Many people move out of cities to rural areas. **Describe the effects** of this migration on the rural areas.

Question 4 (from a Foundation paper)

Look at the two population pyramids.

(a) i) Use the population pyramids to **complete the table below**:

Age	Brazil (LEDC) % male	% female	France (MEDC) % male	% female
10–14	___	6.0	2.7	2.8

   ii) Life expectancy is the average number of years that people are expected to live.

   How does the population pyramid show that people in France have a longer life expectancy than people in Brazil?

   iii) **Suggest two reasons** why there is a difference in life expectancy between France (MEDC) and Brazil (LEDC).

   iv) **Give one piece of evidence** from the population pyramid to show that the birth rate in Brazil is higher than in France.

   v) **Explain** why the birth rate is high in LEDCs such as Brazil.

(b) **With reference to a country which you have studied, describe** what is done to control the rate of population change.

(c) Look again at the population pyramids.

   i) **What does the label 'dependant population' mean**?

   ii) Use the population pyramids to **identify** which countries will complete the following sentence.

   In _____ there is a higher percentage of elderly dependants than in _____ but there is a smaller percentage of young dependants.

   iii) **Describe some ways** by which the dependant population is supported in countries at different levels of economic development, such as France (MEDC) and Brazil (LEDC).

Question 5 (from a Higher paper)

(a) **Study the scatter graph** which shows birth rates and death rates of five countries.

　i) **Which country** has a birth rate of 29 per 1000 and a death rate of 6 per 1000?

　ii) **Which country** has the highest rate of natural population growth?

　iii) **Identify** the relationship shown in the graph between birth rate and death rate.

(b) **Explain** why some LEDCs have high rates of natural population growth.

(c) **Describe** attempts by governments in LEDCs to reduce birth rates.

(d) The population of a country can also change due to international migration. **For an example which you have studied, describe** the reasons for this international migration.

Question 6 (from a Higher paper)

(a) Study the line graph which shows traffic movement in the city of Cambridge.

　i) **Describe what the graph shows** about traffic movement in the city of Cambridge between 1980 and 2000.

　ii) The increase in traffic in urban areas may cause congestion. **How** might traffic congestion impact upon the quality of life in an urban area such as Cambridge?

(b) i) The Metrolink scheme around Manchester, which is shown on the diagram, is part of an 'integrated network' solution to the problem of increasing traffic in urban areas. Use evidence from the diagram to **explain the term**, 'integrated network'.

　ii) **Suggest** three possible problems of developing such a transport network.

(c) **For a named town or city which you have studied, describe** developments which aim to improve the quality of life, such as a regeneration scheme.

Answers to the above tasks

Question 3

a　(i)　Skills
　(ii)　Skills
　(iii)　Skills
　(iv)　Understanding
b　Knowledge
c　Knowledge
d　Understanding and Application

Question 4

(a)　i)　Skills
　ii)　Skills
　iii)　Understanding
　iv)　Skills
　v)　Understanding
(b)　Knowledge
(c)　i)　Knowledge
　ii)　Understanding
　iii)　Understanding and Application

Question 5

(a)　i)　Skills
　ii)　Skills
　iii)　Skills
(b)　Understanding
(c)　Knowledge and Understanding
(d)　Knowledge

Question 6

(a)　i)　Skills
　ii)　Understanding and Application
(b)　i)　Knowledge
　ii)　Understanding
(c)　Knowledge

People and places to live

HOW THE EXAMINERS AWARD THE MARKS

Here are answers to different types of questions. See how examiners give credit for different ideas.

1. Explain why some people in LEDCs have large numbers of children.

Foundation paper question which tests understanding.

Candidate 1's answer

Some people do this because their children keep dying.
Some people do this because they want to ensure that they have someone to look after them when they are older.
Some people do it because the children go out and work for them.
Some people do it to sell their children.

Examiner comment 1

Answer is written in note form, scores 3 marks out of 4, the last point is not credited.

Candidate 2's answer

Due to the poor infant survival rate and the short life expectancy some LEDCs have large numbers of children. These two factors are mainly caused by the country having many droughts and so they lack food and water causing the short infant mortality rate and the short life expectancy.

Examiner comment 2

The answer is grammatically poorly written, it is repetitious, 'short' infant mortality is incorrect, scores 2 marks out of 4 for ideas of poor survival rate of infants and short life expectancy due to the effects of drought.

2. Explain why some LEDCs have high rates of natural population growth.

Higher paper question which tests understanding.

Candidate 3's answer

Some LEDCs have high rates of natural population growth because they don't have the resources to introduce contraceptives. Therefore there are more babies being born. The death rate is fluctuating due to the fact that many people die from disease. This is because the government doesn't have enough money to build good hospitals and have good medical treatment. Even though the death rate is high the birth rate is high which causes a low natural population growth.

Examiner comment 3

The answer scores 2 marks out of 5. It relates high birth rate to high death rate and gives one reason for a high birth rate. The answer goes in to reasons for high death rate which are irrelevant.

Candidate 4's answer

In LEDCs there is a very high birth rate. This is because the people are not very well educated and know little about birth control. In some villages having more children gives families a higher status. Many families have a lot of children to help them farm on the land, many children are required as death rates are high, especially in children. It is tradition that a woman's job is to stay at home and look after children whilst the husband goes to work. When parents get old their children are needed to look after them.

Examiner comment 4

Comprehensive answer, scoring 5 marks out of 5. It explains reasons for high birth rate and relates high birth rate to high death rate.

3. Describe attempts by governments in LEDCs to reduce birth rates.

Foundation paper question testing knowledge and application.

Candidate 5's answer

In China there was a one child policy set up which if any couples have more than one child they are heavily fined. This is because China is a very densely populated country and its amount of natural population growth is high. In theory this attempt should have been successful but it wasn't because people had to choose between the sexes, with most people opting for a boy. This meant that people were discarding unwanted babies so that they would escape fines. The children were still being produced but now they were without parents.

Examiner comment 5

Scores 2 marks out of 4, starting off well by referring to 'one child policy' and how it operates, but the rest of the answer is irrelevant.

Candidate 6's answer

Governments in LEDCs are trying to reduce birth rates in a number of ways. One way is to educate people, especially women. This means women will have more of a choice and may choose not to have children. Centres are set up to educate people about birth control in the hope that birth rates will fall.

By improving health care death rates will fall, and there will be less need for families to have lots of children.

Examiner comment 6

Scores 3 marks out of 4. Three ideas are described well.

Candidate 7's answer

Some attempts made by governments in LEDCs to reduce birth rates are:
– Make contraception free and widely available.
– Educate people about contraception and how to avoid getting pregnant.
– Introduce sterilisation programmes after families have had one or two children.
– Set up good health care services and schools, limit the benefits to families with one or two children.

Examiner comment 7

Scores 4 marks out of 4. Although the answer is in bullet points, the ideas are accurate.

Tasks to do

Now it is your chance to be an examiner! The following answers need marking and you should provide some examiner comments.

4. Study the photograph which shows a squatter settlement. What are the problems of living in such a squatter settlement?

Foundation paper question testing understanding and application, marked out of 4.

People and places to live

Candidate 8's answer

It is dangerous because the houses are too close together and look unstable, it is too crowded and a strong heavy rainfall could probably take off the roof.

Candidate 9's answer

All the houses are crowded and arranged all together. The houses are all damaged and look as if they are going to fall down on top of each other. If one of the houses falls down it will destroy other houses.

Candidate 10's answer

The problems of living in a squatter settlement are the poor standard of living due to the standard of the homes. Homes are very poor quality with little protection from bad weather. Healthcare is poor, homes are so close together that illnesses can be spread very quickly. No space, very crowded with no privacy.

Candidate 11's answer

The problem of living in such a squatter settlement is that there are no modern amenities such as sewage works or rubbish collection. Without these, rubbish and sewage waste are found on the street where it gives off an awful stench and it can cause disease. Without the medicines or health care needed, the people living there can die early from cholera. Also due to dirty, untreated water people who drink it will catch disease.

5. Study the photograph which shows some people building their own house.

To what extent is this a satisfactory solution to the problem of squatter settlements?

Higher paper question testing skills and application, marked out of 4.

Candidate 12's answer

People building their own homes are to an extent better than squatter settlements as they are built of brick so are safer. These houses would be more stable and cleaner as they are not built of bits of tin and anything they can find. These houses would not fall on top of each other as they are stronger.

Candidate 13's answer

The people have a stable roof over their head which is not made from mud and dirt which leaks when it rains. There is more space and there would be a water tank on top to collect water which would not be dirty. Electricity would be in this house whereas before there wasn't any electricity. The houses look more attractive than before and will not smell.

Candidate 14's answer

People building their own homes is a solution to the problem of squatter settlements because the people are building in a different area than the squatter settlement and so would help to move people out. The houses will be safer as they are not so close together and disease won't spread so easily. The house is built of brick with a solid roof to keep out the rain and wind. However, if many people decide to build their own house it could turn the area into another unplanned squatter settlement.

6. What problems are caused for planners and city authorities as a result of many people moving into cities in LEDCs?

Higher paper question testing understanding, marked out of 5.

Candidate 15's answer

The problems that are caused for planners and city authorities are that they become overcrowded. The planners only build centres to hold so many people, with more and more people moving in they cannot cater for them.

Candidate 16's answer

If too many people move to cities in LEDCs the city authorities will have too many people to house and not enough houses.

Jobs will be taken by new people so locals will be out of work.

The city will become more overcrowded and authorities will not be able to move them out to plan new areas for building.

The city will become poor because too many people will need supporting by the authorities, more medicines and schools for example.

Candidate 17's answer

The influx of people into LEDC cities puts a huge strain on the infrastructure of that city with not enough clean water or electricity. The authorities need to be fair to the poorer squatters by developing new housing schemes, but must also keep the powerful and influential richer people happy too. There will be increased demand on doctors and other medical services in the city with thousands of people to each doctor. An increase in crime will stretch the police force and make it harder to combat crime. The new settlers take over unused land by railways or roads or on the outskirts of the city which makes it difficult for the authorities to plan and build new housing developments.

Examiner comments on answers

8. 2/4 poorly expressed
9. 2/4 poorly expressed, two weak ideas
10. 4/4 poorly expressed but four ideas
11. 4/4 comprehensive answer
12. 2/4 not well expressed, two ideas, no reference to what extent
13. 3/4 some ideas may not be accurate but three ideas, still no reference to what extent
14. 4/4 comprehensive answer, with reference to what extent – negative point
15. 2/5 weak ideas
16. 3/5 poorly expressed, but three/four ideas
17. 5/5 comprehensive answer

People and places to live

CASE STUDY ANSWERS

As you have seen there are three different examples of migration which you need to know and each one can be answered by reference to a case study and by making use of a template.

Key ideas

- why people migrate.
- the effect on the area that the people have left.
- the effect on the area that the people go to.
- what people think – attitudes and values.

Why people migrate

Basic idea	More detail – and a question to ask yourself
Not enough land for people	All the fertile land has been used – why?
Shortage of food	Rapid population growth – why?
Climatic hazards	Floods and drought – caused by what?
Poor living conditions	Water supply – what is the evidence?
	Education – what is the evidence?
Jobs	Regular work – why is this better?
	Lots of them – what type of jobs?
Money	Higher wages – compared with whom?

Effect on the area that the people have left

Basic idea	More detail – and a question to ask yourself
Loss of skilled people	The ones who can read and write – why?
The area suffers more decline	Poorest and old people remain – why?

Effect on the area that the people go to

Basic idea	More detail – and a question to ask yourself
A lot of cheap workers	They will work for low wages – why?
Migrants will do jobs which local people will not	Types of job – why will migrants do them?
	Why won't local people do these jobs?
Growth of ethnic communities	Migrants live in the same area – why?

Attitudes and values

Migrants think it is good	New opportunities – what are they?
Migrants have concerns	They feel threatened – why?
Local people think it is good	Better services provided – such as what?
Local people have concerns	They feel threatened – why?

The above example shows how you can make a template in order to include details about international migration from Mexico to USA.

Task to do

Use either the textbook or your own notes to draw a similar template for each of the other types of migration:

- from a rural area to a city in an LEDC [*84–85*].
- from an urban area to a village in the UK [*106–107*].

A reminder of how the case study is marked

If you learn how examiners mark a case study it should help you to write good answers. A case study is marked in 'levels' from level 1 up to level 3. To achieve a higher level answer you will need to give details which are related specifically to your named example. This is shown in the following question.

> Name an area in the UK which has a low population density and explain why it is sparsely populated.
> (5 marks)

Mark scheme

Level 1 (1–2 marks)

Simple statements which attempt to explain low population density, e.g.

- no jobs.
- high land.
- poor climate.

Level 2 (3–4 marks)

More specific statements which explain low population density, e.g.

- few jobs as there are no factories in the area.
- high land is difficult to build settlements on/communications through.
- cold climate/long wet winters.

Level 3 (5 marks)

Uses named example

Detailed and accurate place specific statements, e.g.

- Snowdonia has few jobs as opportunities are limited to sheep farming, forestry, water supply which require few workers.
- highland including many mountains such as Snowdon, which are unsuitable for building.
- poor road communications with winding roads, such as the A5, through mountains.

Tasks to do

Below are three answers. With a partner decide which answer is level 1, 2 and 3. Explain your choice.

Answer 1

Consal, Staffordshire
This area is in the middle of nowhere, it isn't near a big city, no hospital, schools, shops, sources of communication.

Answer 2

North West Scotland
The land in North West Scotland is not suitable for development as the terrain is too rugged to build on, resources are a long way away, the climate isn't very good as it is often wet, it rains all year.
The land in the area is very rough, high and steep with mountains such as Ben Nevis. This allows for very little to be built on the land, that is why it is mainly covered with fell sheep and cattle which can handle the harsh weather.

People and places to live

Answer 3

North Scotland
It is very mountainous which makes the ground not very fertile so not many crops can grow. It also makes it difficult to build houses. Also it is quite cold and wet, making it even harder to grow crops.

Answer 1 is level 1
Answer 2 is level 3
Answer 3 is level 2

The following case study question will also be marked in levels

For an LEDC which you have studied, explain why many people have left rural areas to live in towns and cities. Name either a town or city to which people have moved or the rural area which they have left. (7 marks)

Level 1 (1–3 marks)

Statements including limited detail (simple statements) which explain reasons for rural to urban migration e.g.

- more jobs.
- better services.
- not enough food.

Level 2 (4–6 marks)

More developed (detailed) statements which explain reasons for rural to urban migration, e.g.

- more jobs in cities where they can work in the informal sector/factories.
- greater access to schools/hospitals/clinics.
- people can buy food from markets rather than rely on unproductive farmland.

Level 3 (7 marks)

Uses named example.

Comprehensive, accurate and place specific statements, e.g.

- They can make money in the informal sector by selling fruit to tourists on Rio de Janeiro's famous beaches.
- They can work as shoe shiners in Placa de Se and Placa de Republica, the two main squares in the city centre of Sao Paulo.
- Sao Paulo offers hope such as in the Cinqua Pora development where basic concrete houses are being built with piped water and sewage pipes, even in the favelas which have developed on the steep hillsides. The people have better access to health care and education than in the countryside.
- People living in the valley of the Sao Francisco River lost their farmland when dams and reservoirs were built along it for HEP generation, so they moved to the city.

Remember: these are all different ways that your answer can be made 'place specific'. You do not need to include more than one reference to real place details to make your answer level 3, if it contains enough developed ideas.

Tasks to do

Below are three examples of answers marked at the different levels along with an explanation by the examiner of why they got this level. Discuss the examiner comments with a partner to make sure you both understand why they have been marked at this level.

Level 1 answer

I studied Nairobi in Kenya where people have moved from rural to urban because there have not been good prospects for the young people in the rural area so they have moved. They think that life in a big town is brilliant and they will earn lots of money. Also the people who have moved have no income and have to search for work in Nairobi. Their friends and family might already be there so they may want to be with them.

Examiner comment

This answer is marked at level 1 because it is made up of a number of simple ideas. To make these ideas into a level 2 answer they need to be developed, for example **why** there are poor prospects in the rural area, **how** they will earn lots of money in the city.

Level 2 answer

In Lima, Peru, many people have left the surrounding villages to try to improve their quality of life. This is because the villagers are usually tenants on someone else's land so they have no reason to improve the land as they farm on it. They also have to give some of their produce to the landowner. There is no guarantee of food when you are a subsistence farmer so if there is a bad year then you and your family may starve.

In the city there is a higher chance of work. As you live in a squatter settlement you own your house and so want to improve it. The communities are very close knit so you can often find help. Often there are friends or relatives living in the city that can help or advise you. In Lima there are more basic services such as pumped water, electricity and rubbish collection. This encourages people to move to the city as they don't exist in the countryside. There are more jobs in Lima and the chance of a factory job where you can get a guaranteed wage. There are more middle class people so if you worked in the informal sector then you could work for them shining shoes or cleaning cars. You could also steal from them. There are more bright lights in Lima so it is easier to have fun (bars, clubs).

Examiner comment

This is a good level 2 answer. Both 'push' and 'pull' factors are developed. To make this into a level 3 answer some real place details need to be included, for example names of villages, named industries where people can get employment, or locations in Lima where they may go to find customers for shining shoes.

Level 3 answer

In Mexico there is much rural to urban migration as Mexico City is now the most highly populated city in the world and there is massive migration to the capital city from the rural areas each year. There are many reasons why people want to move to Mexico City from the surrounding rural areas. There are push factors which make people want to move such as less jobs in rural areas and less opportunities. Farming a small area of land would not provide enough food to sell or make a profit on and sometimes not enough to feed the family if there was a drought. Maybe a relative lives in the city and there are job opportunities in new businesses. Many people dream of getting a job in the famous Zona Rose, the CBD of Mexico City but most end up working as unskilled labourers on building sites and living in shanty towns such as 'La Esperazo' on the edge of Mexico City. Even living here people can earn money in the city to send back to their families in rural areas.

Examiner comment

This is a level 3 answer because it contains developed ideas about why people move to the city **and** includes 'real place' details about Mexico City.

> **Remember:** a good way to check that your answer is level 3 is to cover up the name of the example. Are there other details which will tell the examiner that you are writing about a 'real' place?

three
People and their Needs

This unit is divided into three sections:

- Quality of Life
- Economic Activities
- Energy

Only the Economic Activities section is included in the Short Course Specification.

QUALITY OF LIFE

The **quality of life** section can be divided into three parts:

1. Wealth is not evenly spread across the world

In some countries the average person has a short life expectancy, the health of the people is poor and there is not enough wealth for the people to be well fed or educated.

You will need to revise:

- how and why quality of life varies between countries which are at different levels of development. [129]
- how different indicators can be used to measure quality of life. [130–133]

You will need to be able to use maps, graphs and figures which show differences between the quality of life of people who live in different countries. You could be asked to use:

- a map of the world or one continent showing differences in one indicator of quality of life (e.g. GDP, life expectancy, infant mortality, literacy, nutrition). [129 130]
- bar graphs or tables showing the values of different indicators. [129]
- a scatter graph showing the relationship between two different indicators. [131]

You may be asked to complete the shading used on a map or plot information on a graph. Alternatively, you could be asked to describe and suggest reasons for the patterns and relationships shown.

Remember: look carefully at the map, graph or figures and support your answer by quoting precise and accurate details from them. Don't forget to give the units (such as km). They will be labelled on the axis of the graph or in the key of the map. If you are asked to plot something, do so with care. Use a ruler to measure accurately, rather than just guessing.

2. Employment structure

Employment structure is about the proportions of the working population employed in different types of industry. You should be able to compare the employment structure of different countries. You are likely to be given graphs or figures which show the percentage of people employed in different types of industries in two or more countries.

You will need to revise:

- what the term 'employment structure' means and what is meant by primary, secondary and tertiary industry.
- examples of each type of industry.
- how and why employment structure varies between countries.
- how and why the employment structure of a country is likely to change over time. [134–135]

Remember: look carefully at the wording of the questions. If you are asked about the differences in employment structure between countries, it is no good writing about just one of them. Try to use words like 'whereas' or 'more/less' so you can compare effectively.

FIGURE 17

Time line/living graph

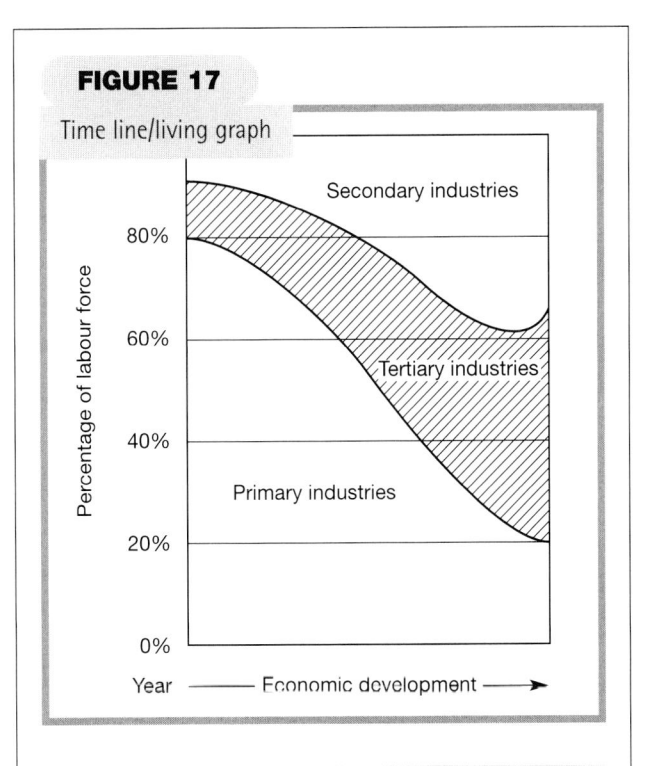

[Graph showing percentage of labour force (0%-80%+) vs Year / Economic development, with three bands: Primary industries, Secondary industries, and Tertiary industries]

Labels to place on the graph:

- Most people work on farms
- Financial sector and tourist industry grows with increasing wealth
- Declining employment in factories as many manufactured goods are imported
- Service sector grows as the government can afford to provide services such as education and health care
- Mechanisation reduces workforce on farms
- Heavy industry grows up using local raw materials
- Coal mining begins on a large scale

Time line/living graph – employment structure as an indicator of economic development

Here is a graph which shows how the percentages employed in the primary, secondary and tertiary sectors have changed in MEDCs such as the UK over the last two centuries. The employment structure of a country can be used as an indicator of economic development. If you put these labels on the graph at the correct periods of time, it will help you to learn why the employment structure of a country changes as it develops.

3. Industry in an LEDC

You will need to have studied how and why industry has grown rapidly in one LEDC.

Such countries are often referred to as Newly Industrialised Countries (NICs). A popular example is South Korea [138–139] but there are lots of other examples (e.g. Taiwan and Singapore). For your case study you will need to revise:

- how and why industry has grown rapidly in the country and how this has caused the employment structure to change.
- the effects of the growth of industry in the country. These are likely to include both benefits and disadvantages to both people and natural environment.

Remember: it is important that you make the correct choice of case study. You will not gain full marks by choosing a country like the UK or USA (which are **not** LEDCs) or by choosing a country like Ethiopia or Sudan (where industry is **not** growing rapidly).

Use the case study of South Korea [PRD 138-139] or your own notes to write as many statements as you can on cards about the **causes** and **consequences** of rapid industrial growth in this 'Tiger Economy'.

Some could be facts which help explain the **causes** of rapid industrial growth: e.g. Trans National Companies (TNCs) were attracted to South Korea by low production costs.

Others could be the **consequences** of growth: e.g. more people migrated to towns and cities to get jobs in factories.

Write each set of statements on revision cards so you will be able to learn them. If you colour code your revision cards, this should help you to remember the difference between causes and consequences.

Remember: in case study questions on this topic, you could be asked about either the causes or the consequences of growth, or both. Also remember that the consequences will include both good and bad. If you are asked to write about both, you must make sure you do so in order to reach the highest level of response. Develop all the points you make. Don't write lists of simple ideas like noise, pollution, jobs, money and traffic.

People and their Needs

ECONOMIC ACTIVITIES

The **economic activities** section is divided into three parts:

1. Agriculture

Agriculture is the growing of crops and production of animal products for food and other raw materials. You will need to know the following:

- what 'subsistence' and 'commercial' farming mean. [140]
- the reasons why different types of farming take place in different areas. [141–147]
- how and why farming in either the UK or the EU is changing. [148–151]

You must have two case studies, one of a subsistence farming system (in an LEDC) and one of a commercial farming system (in either the UK or EU). In your case studies you need to learn how the land is used in each area and understand why it is used in the way it is. There are lots of examples of commercial and subsistence farming systems to choose from. Dairy farming in North Yorkshire is an example of commercial farming and rice farming in India is an example of subsistence farming. [141–147]. You should be able to explain how the following factors affect the way the land is used:

Physical factors: e.g. climate, relief of the land, soil fertility, size of the farm/fields.

Economic factors: e.g. demand for crops and animal products, prices that crops or animals can be sold for, cost and availability of workers, availability of machinery, cost of land, ease of access to markets.

Political factors: e.g. government policies such as grants and quotas.

> **Remember:** do not get mixed up between commercial and subsistence farming. A farming **system** will have inputs, processes and outputs. Make sure you learn these carefully for both of your case studies.

Diagram sequence – impacts of changing farming

Changes in farming since the 1940s have led to increased water pollution. Rivers and lakes in agricultural areas are sometimes polluted as large amounts of fertilizer and other chemicals are used.

Eutrophication of water in a river or lake can occur when too many nutrients (such as nitrates from fertilizers) become dissolved in the water. Runoff of rain water from the farmland may carry nitrates to nearby rivers and lakes. These nitrates help organisms like algae to grow. This reduces oxygen which is needed by the life forms in the lake to survive.

It is helpful to remember a process by using a series of simple diagrams to show the different stages. Try drawing the sequence of simple pictures or symbols to help you to remember the process of eutrophication.

- tractor (spreading fertilizer).
- rain (washing nitrates off the land).
- algae (growing in the river).
- oxygen (being used up).
- fish (floating on the surface).

So learn TRACTOR ... RAIN ... ALGAE ... OXYGEN ... FISH.

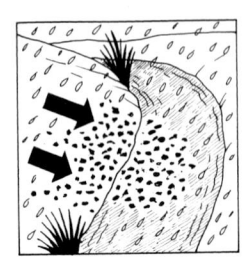

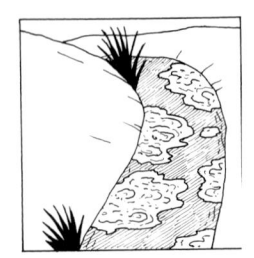

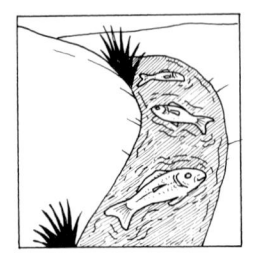

Mind maps – Farming

Here is the start of a mind map to help you to summarise what you know about agriculture. Use your notes or [📖 140-151] to help you to add details around each box.

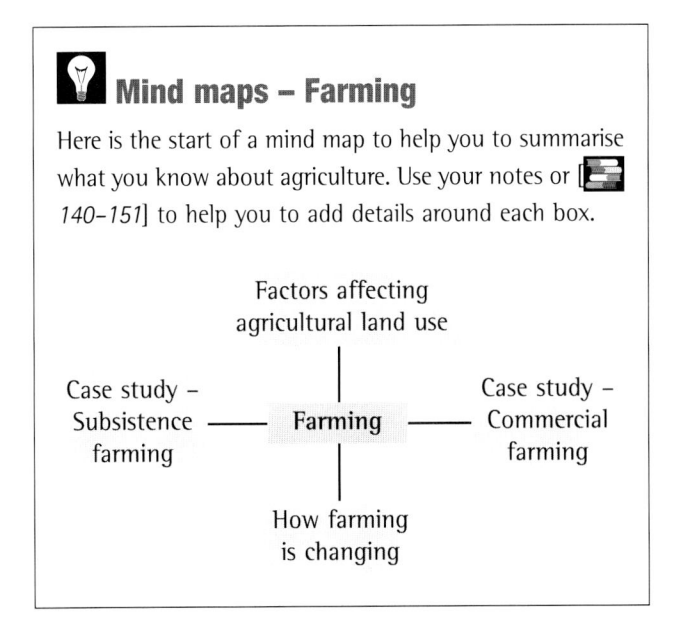

```
              Factors affecting
              agricultural land use
                      |
Case study –          |          Case study –
Subsistence ——— Farming ——— Commercial
  farming             |            farming
                      |
                How farming
                 is changing
```

2. Manufacturing and distribution industries

These involve the processing or assembly of finished products (manufacturing) along with their dispatch to where they are sold and used (distribution). You will need to know the following:

- what is meant by manufacturing and distribution industries.
- the factors which attract industry to certain types of location. [📖 152-155]

You must have two case studies, one of a manufacturing industry and one of a distribution industry, each in the UK. In your case studies you need to learn where the industries are located and be able to explain why the locations were chosen. There are lots of examples of case studies of industries to choose from. One must be an example of a manufacturing industry, such as the Lynemouth aluminium smelter in Northumberland and the other must be an example of a distribution industry, such as the Argos distribution warehouse at Stafford. [📖 153]

You should be able to explain how the following factors have influenced the location of industry:

- the site – the space available and cost of the land, along with the relief of the land.
- raw materials and power supplies – the type of raw materials and sources of power available and from where they are obtained, whether they are bulky or perishable.
- markets – where the products are sold and what methods of transport are available.
- labour – the cost and availability of workers with appropriate skills.
- political factors – the impact of Government and EU policies such as the availability of grants.
- environmental factors – the environmental impacts of some types of industries may make it difficult for planning permission to be obtained in some areas (e.g. in National Parks), whilst other locations may attract industry because of their pleasant environments (e.g. greenfield sites).

Remember: when you explain why industries grew up in certain places you need to expand each of your ideas. Don't just state that 'it is near the M6 motorway' but explain the importance of this by pointing out that 'the location close to the M6 motorway makes it easy to transport raw materials to the factory and finished products to the market'.

Memory maps – location of industry

Look at a diagram of factors which influence the location of industry. [📖 152]

You should be able to draw a diagram such as this using your case studies of manufacturing and distribution industries. For example if you were using the Lynemouth aluminium smelter as your case study [📖 154-155], the label for raw materials would read 'Bauxite from Australia, Guinea and Jamaica'. Complete diagrams for your case studies making sure that you fully understand the reasons for their locations.

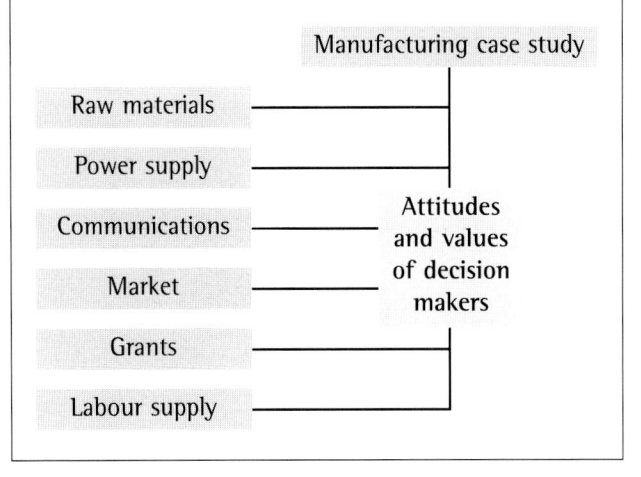

```
                        Manufacturing case study
Raw materials     ———
Power supply      ———
Communications    ———    Attitudes
                         and values
Market            ———    of decision
                         makers
Grants            ———
Labour supply     ———
```

People and their Needs

3. Tourism

This is an economic activity which is growing in importance in many parts of the world. Whilst tourism can create wealth in an area it can create problems for both people and the natural environment. You must know two case studies, one of an area where tourism is important in an LEDC and one in a country from the EU.

> **Remember:** one of these case studies has to be from an EU country but you cannot choose somewhere from in the UK. Name the area of your case study as precisely as you can rather than just naming the country (e.g. Costa del Sol in Spain).

In each of your case studies you need to learn:

- why tourism has become important in the area.
- what the benefits and problems of tourism are to the local people and natural environment.
- what strategies can be used to manage tourism in a sustainable way.

> **Remember:** sustainability involves the use of the natural environment and resources in such a way that it will not be destroyed for future generations.

There are lots of examples of areas you could choose, where tourism is important. You may have studied Menorca as an example from the EU and Kenya as an example from an LEDC. [156–159]

ENERGY

The **energy** section looks at how the increasing demand for energy is being satisfied and the impacts of changes in supplies of fuel and power for domestic and industrial use.

You need to know about:

- the different types of fuel and power which can be used.
- the difference between renewable and non-renewable energy sources.
- the reasons for the changing importance of different fuels in the UK, in particular, the reduction in the use of fossil fuels.
- how to ensure that energy supplies in the UK are sustainable, in particular, by the use of alternative renewable energy sources.
- the debate over the use of nuclear energy. [160–163]

> Are you finding it helpful to use lists of letters to learn things?
>
> How about this geographical mnemonic for the forms of energy which are 'alternatives' to fossil fuels?
>
> **W**ave power
> **E**lectricity (hydro)
> **S**olar power
> **T**idal power
> **N**uclear power
> **W**ind power
>
> So remember **WEST NW** (a compass direction) which is a **geographical** link which might help you to remember another alternative form of energy (**g**eothermal power).

You need to know a case study of an area or settlement which has been affected by changes in energy production. It could have been affected by the growth of energy production in the area (e.g. where a new opencast coal mine has been opened) or it could have been affected by decline in production of a source of energy in the area (e.g. the closure of a nuclear power station). Your example can be from the UK or any other MEDC and you need to learn:

- the reasons for the changes which have taken place in the area which you have chosen.
- the effects of the changes on the people who live there and on the economy.

Remember: **social effects** are the effects on the people, **economic effects** involve the impacts on wealth in the area.

An example is Holmewood in Derbyshire, where the closure of the coalmine affected the local community in both positive and negative ways. [164–165]

Remember: do not assume that all effects of changes in an area will be bad ones. A balanced answer will include details about both the **benefits and disadvantages** of the change which has taken place and consider effects on both people (social effects) and the economy (economic effects).

CASE STUDY ANSWERS

Question:

For a distribution industry which you have studied, describe and explain its location.

Name of case study:
Prolog distribution warehouse.

Location:
Alongside Junction 27 of the M1 motorway close to the village of Annesley, in Nottinghamshire, which is in the East Midlands.

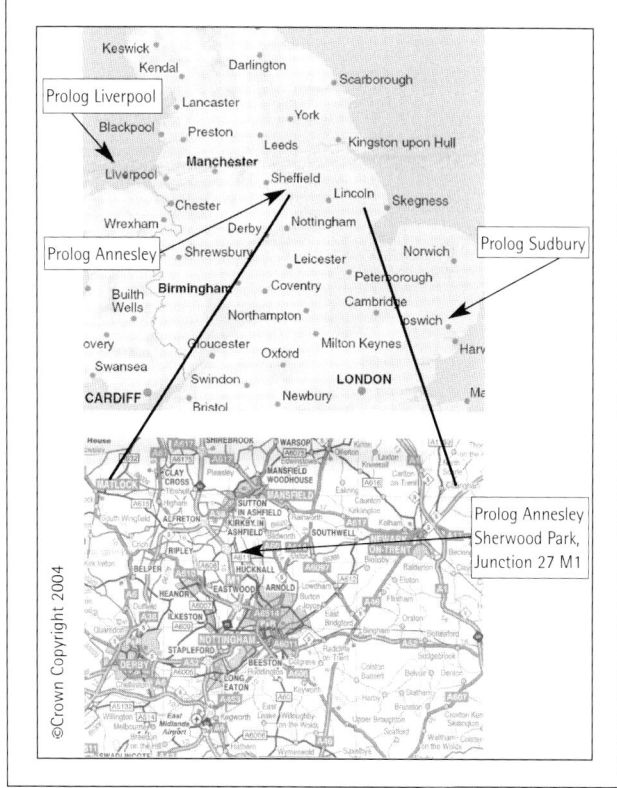

Word games – Energy

This grid contains words which you learned when you studied energy. It also contains the names of places which fit with the words. [160–165] Can you sort them into four groups and explain why you have grouped each set of words together?

Holmewood	turbine	reprocessing	natural gas	radiation
solar	Royd Moor	geothermal	fission	coal
uranium	lignite	oil	national grid	wave
cooling tower	generator	Sutton Bridge	tidal	Sellafield

Why not try to write a grid of words and places connected with the following and ask a friend to sort them into groups? Make sure that you discuss any on which you do not agree.

Tourism   Manufacturing industry   Distribution industry

People and their Needs

Prolog is a distribution company with three sites in the UK – Sudbury (in Suffolk), Haydock (near Liverpool) and Sherwood Park, Annesley (Nottinghamshire). Prolog's customers include a number of very large government departments, (such as the Department for Education and Skills) and companies (such as the RAC and NTL Home). These organisations require Prolog to collect and then store large quantities of material in warehouses and to assemble it carefully for mailing throughout the UK. In the case of the DfES, over half a million mailings are sent each year ranging in size from single letters to bulk mail to every school and every teacher in the country. For the RAC, Prolog send individual envelopes requested by telephone and bulk mail to all members. To succeed in this Prolog needs to operate for 24 hours a day throughout the week and needs excellent access to the motorway network to collect materials and send out deliveries. All Prolog's customers require orders to be completed quickly.

Further details on Prolog's customers can be found at: http://www.prolog.uk.com/case_studies/index.html

This case study requires an understanding of the reasons why Prolog decided to locate a new distribution centre in Nottinghamshire in 1996 and subsequently expand it considerably, with five warehouses now employing over 700 full time workers (at peak times this rises to 1500). The warehousing and distribution is mainly done by men, whilst the packing is female dominated.

This part of England has experienced significant employment change in the last few years with the closure of many coalmines and factories. Those factories that have survived have often reduced their labour force as new machinery has been developed and new employment has often been in small units, compared to the coalmines and factories which often used to employ over 1000 workers. As a result, unemployment became a significant problem and Nottinghamshire County Council were keen to encourage new employment in this area.

Prolog chose Sherwood Park for their new distribution centre for a number of reasons. This is a central location in the United Kingdom between the existing two centres at Sudbury (to the South East) and Haydock near Liverpool (to the North West). The Sherwood Park site is next to Junction 27 on the M1, which enables lorries to access the whole of the United Kingdom using the motorway network, and allows workers to travel in easily from the surrounding towns. In this area many other distribution and warehouse companies also have centres nearby and the East Midlands Airport can be reached in about 20 minutes by road for international distribution by air.

With increased unemployment in the region, there were a number of Government incentives available. The area was an Enterprise Zone which helped Prolog in a number of ways such as not having to pay rent or business rates for a period of time. In addition to this a grant of over £500,000 was given by the Department of Trade and Industry, along with a job creation grant from Nottinghamshire County Council.

The Sherwood Park development is huge and offered plenty of space for future expansion and, as only the second firm on the site after Kodak, Prolog was able to choose the sites for its warehouses. The Park itself is a gently sloping greenfield site (so building costs were low) and it is in a pleasant rural environment yet near to several urban settlements from which to draw a workforce.

How to describe the location of a place

You could be asked to describe the location of a place on any of the examination papers. In this unit this could be the location of a farm, factory, area where tourism is important or a village where a mine or power station has recently opened or closed down. On Paper 1 or 2 you are likely to have to do this using your case study knowledge so it is wise to learn, in as much detail as possible, the locations of all your case studies. On Paper 3 and 4, you could be given a map and asked to describe a location. This question tests your map interpretation skills.

Whenever you describe a location you need to:

- Name the area in which your case study is located.
  The Prolog distribution warehouse is located in the county of Nottinghamshire which is in the East Midlands.

- Name the settlement in which the case study is located. If the settlement is large, say precisely where it is in the settlement.
  Prolog is located on the western edge of the village of Annesley, between the village and the M1 motorway.

- If there are any roads close by to help locate the case study, identify them by their numbers.
  Prolog is located alongside the A608 close to its junction with the M1 motorway.

- Give details of the distance and direction of the case study from any larger towns and cities in the area.
  Prolog is located between Nottingham, the centre of which is 16 km to the SSE, and Mansfield, which is 13 km to the NNE. It is 5 km north west of the former coal mining town of Hucknall.

Remember: be as precise as possible and include as much detail as you can. For the other case studies which you will learn for this unit, describe and learn their locations using the four ideas above.

The case studies will always be marked using 'levels'. Remember this means that a detailed answer, which includes specific information about the place, will always gain more marks than one which could really be about anywhere. A level 3 answer needs to include specific place details and the points made should be developed fully. Whilst an examiner would not expect you to include every reason for the choice of location, you should always try to include as many as you can, and at least three different ideas.

Tasks to do

Below are three answers which use the Prolog case study. Which do you think gives the most detailed explanation of the reasons for the location at Annesley? Does it also include specific information about the place or could it be about anywhere?

Which answer gives place details but does not develop the ideas to explain the location? Try to improve the answers so they would all reach level 3.

Question:

For a distribution industry which you have studied, describe and explain its location.

Answer 1

Prolog is a distribution industry which is located near the M1 in Nottinghamshire. It distributes booklets and other materials all over the country. It is a good location because it is near the M1 and there is enough space. It is a greenfield site and there are lots of towns and cities nearby.

Answer 2

The Prolog distribution warehouse was built in the East Midlands, the central location was a good one so that they could send materials by road easily to all parts of the country. It is near the M1 motorway so lorries do not have to queue in traffic for long before they can get on the motorway. The warehouse is built on a greenfield site which is gently sloping. This made costs relatively low and the environment is pleasant for the workforce.

Answer 3

Prolog is a distribution warehouse at Annesley, which is in the East Midlands between Mansfield and Nottingham. It is built close to Junction 27 of the M1. It is between their other distribution centres at Sudbury and Liverpool.

The location was chosen because of the communications and the fact that it is a greenfield site in an Enterprise Zone.

People and their Needs

Task to do

Use your notes to complete a case study for the following question:

> Name an area in the EU where tourism is important. Describe how tourism is being managed to reduce the problems caused by visitors.

You could use either your own notes or the case study of Menorca. [*156–157*] You may be able to add details by looking at websites using a search engine such as: http://www.google.com/ Use key words for your search such as 'Menorca', 'Balearic', 'tourism', 'sustainable' and 'management'. You should be able to find out about the Environment Tax (eco-tax) which was used in Menorca between May 2002 and November 2003.

This article was taken from the website of Tourism Concern at http://www.tourismconcern.org.uk/ You should be able to add some ideas to your notes from it.

Balearic Islands introduce eco-tax?

16 Feb 2002

Tourism Concern press statement

To the delight of local people and environmental campaigners in the Balearics, a long-awaited eco-tax on tourists will finally come into force on 1 May 2002.

All visitors to the islands staying in hotels will pay an average of €1 (62 pence) per day, and it is hoped that €60,000 per year will be raised to tackle the environmental havoc that years of unregulated tourism have wreaked in the islands. Planned projects for the fund include destroying some of the eyesore high rise hotels that have come to symbolise all that is bad about Balearic tourist development.

Sustainable tourism campaigning organisation, Tourism Concern, has been consulting with local environmental organisations ever since 30,000 people marched on Majorca's capital, Palma, 3 years ago, demanding a halt to all further tourism developments.

'The Balearic government, local people and environmental groups are certain that the eco-tax is necessary in order to give them hope of protecting the region's ecosystem and vital resources such as water. We feel that operators and tourists should respect that,' says Director of Tourism Concern, Patricia Barnett.

Hazel Morgan, spokesperson for Ibiza's Amics de la Terra (Friends of the Earth), agrees with the UK tour operators that a fall in visitor numbers is possible. But Morgan says that this wouldn't be such a bad thing.

'We need to reduce visitor numbers – the islands are at saturation point,' says Morgan.

'Every year, more people come, putting more pressure on scarce resources, but there is less and less money because the packages just keep getting cheaper. Something needs to change because if our environment is not protected, the Balearics will simply end up as another Benidorm.'

Remember: include specific details about the place which you choose and answer in as much detail as possible.

DIFFERENT TYPES OF RESOURCES

The question papers contain different types of resources which aim to test what you understand and can do. Each question will contain one or more resources such as:

- maps of different types and scales (e.g. world maps showing the distribution of an activity, Ordnance Survey maps).
- graphs of different types (e.g. bar, pie, line, divided rectangles, scatter graphs and triangular graphs).
- photographs, (including aerial photographs) and satellite images.
- cartoons.
- tables of figures.

All examination questions at both Foundation and Higher tier contain a variety of the above types, and some resources, particularly on Papers 3 and 4 may be used in several questions.

The following examination questions show how different resources about Prolog can be used in a question about distribution industry.

Describe the main features of the Prolog distribution warehouse shown in the photograph. (3)

Remember: look at the mark allocation for the question which will be in brackets. If the question is worth four marks or less it will be **point marked**. This means that the examiner will give you a mark for each correct statement which you write. You will only need to make three points if it is worth three marks. Which three features of the building shown on page 46 could you describe? Remember to be as **precise** as possible.

Use Figure 19 to describe the main differences between the employment structure of Mansfield and the UK. (2)

Figure 19

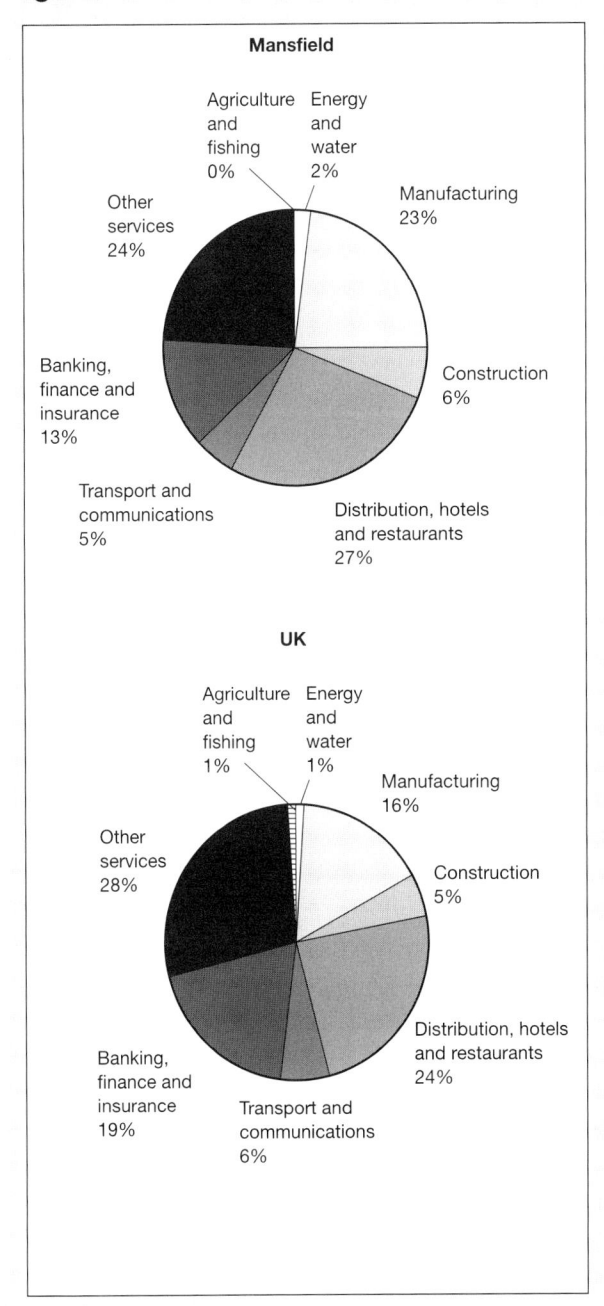

Mansfield:
- Agriculture and fishing 0%
- Energy and water 2%
- Manufacturing 23%
- Construction 6%
- Distribution, hotels and restaurants 27%
- Transport and communications 5%
- Banking, finance and insurance 13%
- Other services 24%

UK:
- Agriculture and fishing 1%
- Energy and water 1%
- Manufacturing 16%
- Construction 5%
- Distribution, hotels and restaurants 24%
- Transport and communications 6%
- Banking, finance and insurance 19%
- Other services 28%

Remember: if you are asked to describe the differences you must write about both Mansfield and the UK. It will help if you use words like 'higher/lower' or 'whereas' (e.g. there is a **higher** percentage employed in manufacturing in Mansfield than in the UK overall, **whereas** there is a **lower** percentage employed in banking finance and insurance).

Task to do

The Paper 1 question below is about tourism in an LEDC. Look at how the resources are used.

5. Study Fig. 20.

Figure 20

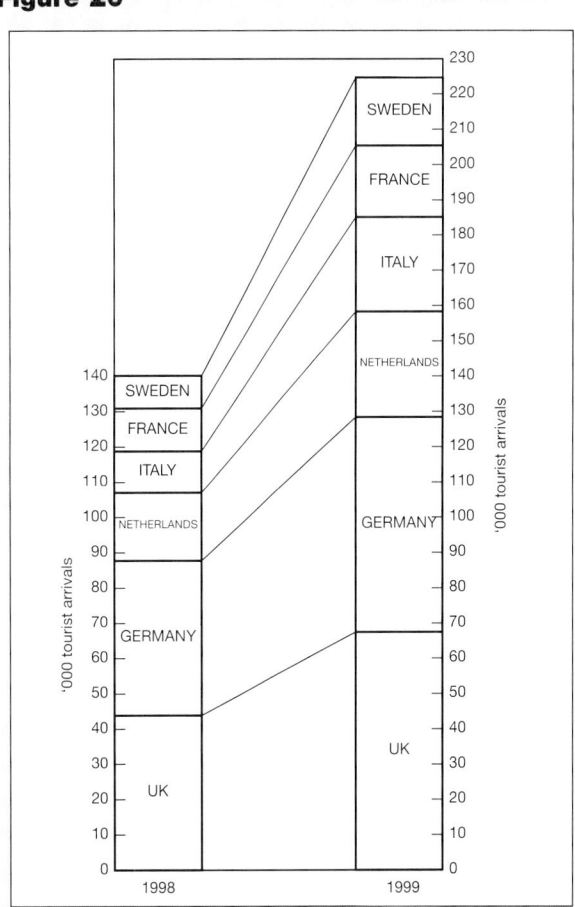

1998 ('000 tourist arrivals):
- SWEDEN ~130
- FRANCE ~120
- ITALY ~110
- NETHERLANDS ~100
- GERMANY ~60
- UK ~20

1999 ('000 tourist arrivals):
- SWEDEN ~220
- FRANCE ~200
- ITALY ~170
- NETHERLANDS ~140
- GERMANY ~100
- UK ~35

a) Fill in the gaps in the following sentences.

Bali is an LEDC which is a popular tourist destination. It is an island in SE Asia. Most of the tourists who visit LEDCs such as Bali are from more _____ countries. Between 1998 and 1999 the number of tourists to Bali from the six European countries _____ (e.g. in 1998 there were 9000 tourists from Sweden but in 1999 there were _____ tourists from Sweden). (3)

People and their Needs

b) Study the photographs which show different attractions in Bali

   i) Identify one photograph which shows a natural attraction and one which shows a human attraction. (1)

D

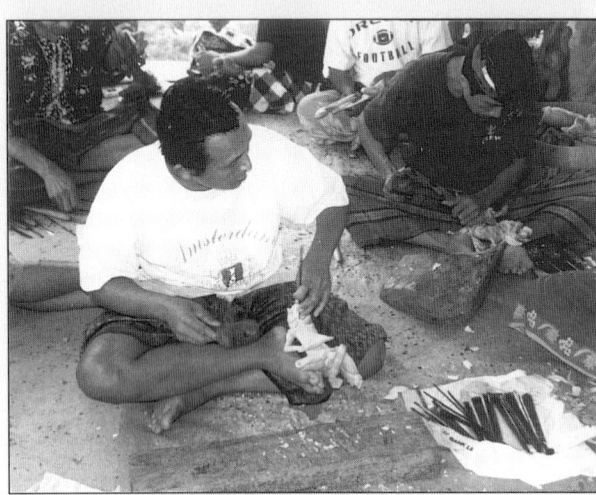

E

F

G

   ii) Explain the attraction for tourists in each of the photographs you have chosen. (2)

   iii) Give three effects of tourism on the lives of people who live in LEDCs like Bali. (4)

Look at the answers to these questions from three candidates along with the resources.

Candidate A

20 a) Bali is an LEDC which is a popular tourist destination. It is an island in SE Asia. Most of the tourists who visit LEDCs such as Bali are from more DEVELOPED countries. Between 1998 and 1999 the number of tourists to Bali from the six European countries INCREASED (e.g. in 1998 there were 9000 tourists from Sweden but in 1999 there were 225,000 tourists from Sweden).

b) (i) Natural attraction photo F
        Human attraction photo G

(ii) F White sandy beaches, clear oceans and hot weather.
G Mysterious temple built by different cultures in a hot place, tourists may find it interesting.

(iii) 1. It creates employment – people to work in bars, e.g. waitresses.
2. It may lead to building a tourist attraction near people's houses, making the people have more crowded lives.
3. Boat trips or any water sports could affect fishing which the people who live there need to do to get food for their families.

Candidate B

20 a) Bali is an LEDC which is a popular tourist destination. It is an island in SE Asia. Most of the tourists who visit LEDCs such as Bali are from more WEALTHY countries. Between 1998 and 1999 the number of tourists to Bali from the six European countries WENT UP (e.g. in 1998 there were 9000 tourists from Sweden but in 1999 there were 225,000 tourists from Sweden).

b) i) Natural attraction photo D
       Human attraction photo E

ii) D Because mountain climbers go there to climb the mountains.
E This would attract people because it shows people living in a community and they could watch new arts and crafts.

iii) 1. There will be noise pollution from planes and extra traffic.
2. Tourism will bring in money so new buildings such as hospitals will be built.
3. Tourists intrude on their habitat which the Bali people don't like their privacy destroyed.

Candidate C

20 a) Bali is an LEDC which is a popular tourist destination. It is an island in SE Asia. Most of the tourists who visit LEDCs such as Bali are from more EUROPEAN countries. Between 1998 and 1999 the number of tourists to Bali from the six European countries WAS HIGH (e.g. in 1998 there were 9000 tourists from Sweden but in 1999 there were 225 tourists from Sweden).

b) (i) Natural attraction photo F
        Human attraction photo G

(ii) F Because it shows a beautiful beach.
G As it shows great man-made buildings.

(iii) 1. The rain forests are chopped down.
2. The place becomes busier.
3. There is more pollution.

The examiner would give full marks to candidates A and B. Even though these two candidates have answered the questions in different ways, you will be able to see why they were given the marks. They have used the resources to give accurate responses and given full answers and explanations.

Candidate C however has been several errors. Can you find them all?

▸ In Section a) they score no marks. Neither of the first 2 words which they have inserted make sense and their figure of 225 is wrong as they have ignored the facts that the graph scale is in 000's.

▸ In Section b) ii they have made little use of either photograph. They could have used a better descriptive word than 'beautiful' for the beach (e.g. sandy, white, deserted, tropical) and they could have described the 'great man made buildings', perhaps identifying them as temples or referring to the ornate carvings.

▸ In section b) iii the information about the rainforest is not relevant as this question is asking about effects on the lives of people. They make no attempt to develop the ideas of 'busier' and 'pollution' which will not score marks unless they are more specific.

four

People and the Environment

This unit is divided into two sections which look at the impacts of people on:

- the local environment.
- the global environment.

The section on the local environment does not mean that examples have to be used from your local area, however the examples have to be at a small (local) scale. In the section on the global environment, you need to be able to understand how people can cause environmental impacts to the entire world.

The section on the global environment is included in the Short Course Specification along with the section on tropical rain forests.

LOCAL ENVIRONMENT

The **local environment** section is divided into four parts:

1. The extraction of raw materials

This requires you to know a case study of a mine or quarry in an MEDC. [180–181]

You will need to learn:

a) the name of your case study area and its location

b) the benefits of the mine or quarry to the local people and economy.

c) the ways in which the mine or quarry damages the environment.

d) conflicts which are caused by the mine or quarry.

> **Remember:** read the question carefully. Is it asking you about the impacts of the mine or quarry on the local people or on the natural environment? You will only score high marks for your case study answer if you answer the question **fully** and give **details** about your named area.

There are many environmental impacts of mining or quarrying. These include:

- **Visual intrusion** Mines and quarries are often unpleasant to look at and can be seen from miles away as they cover large areas and often have ugly surface buildings.

- **Atmospheric pollution** Dust is likely to get into the air when the rocks are extracted and the large vehicles used release exhaust fumes into the atmosphere.

- **Noise pollution** Quarries are noisy because the rocks are often extracted by blasting or by using large cutting machines. Heavy lorries which remove materials from both mines and quarries are often noisy.

- **Loss of vegetation** When land is quarried, any plants growing on the land will be removed to get at the rock underneath. This could threaten not just species of plants but entire ecosystems which depend on them.

- **Water pollution** When rain falls on areas which are being mined or quarried, waste is often washed into local rivers and lakes. Sometimes chemicals used can pollute local rivers too.

> **Remember:** never use the word 'pollution' without expanding on it. What type of pollution does it cause and how is that damaging the local environment?

Mind maps – Mining/quarrying

Here is a mind map to help you to learn about the extraction of raw materials. What case study do you have for a mine or quarry? You need to know about the opportunities, conflicts and environmental costs of the mine or quarry which you have studied. In this mind map, there are three ideas for each. Can you add more, making sure they fit with your example?

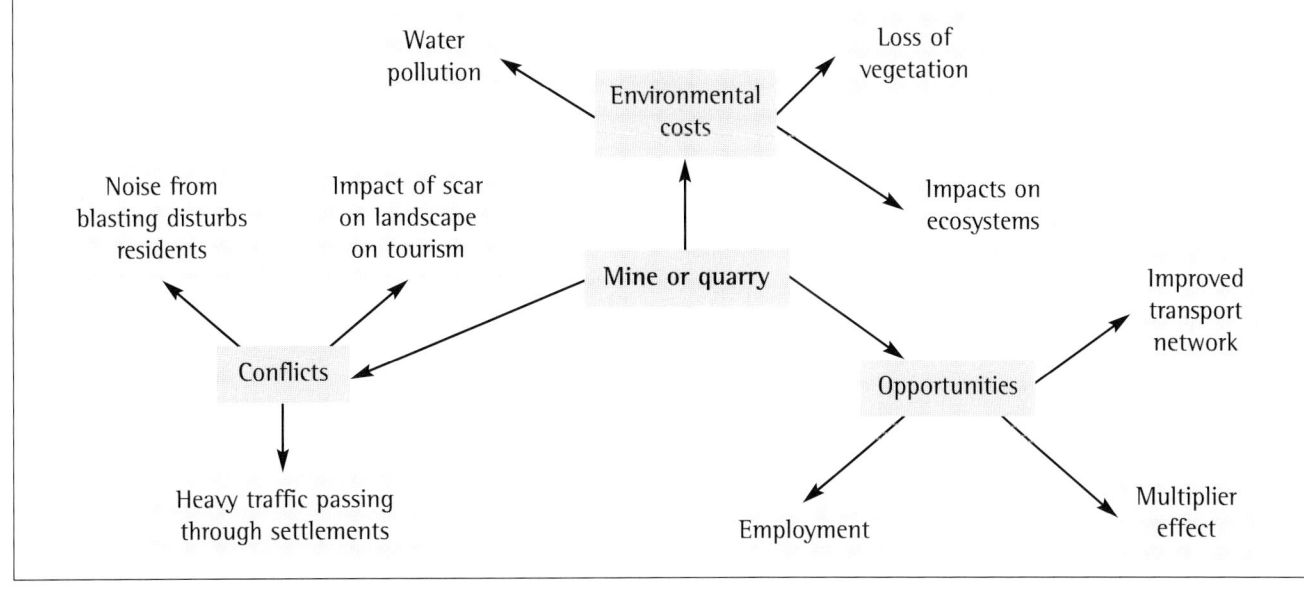

```
                    Water              Loss of
                   pollution          vegetation
                       ↖  Environmental ↗
                           costs
                             ↑
   Noise from     Impact of scar        Impacts on
   blasting disturbs  on landscape      ecosystems
   residents         on tourism
       ↖              ↗                           Improved
         ↖          ↗                             transport
          Conflicts ← Mine or quarry →            network
             ↓                    Opportunities ↗
                                        ↙      ↘
      Heavy traffic passing                     Multiplier
      through settlements      Employment        effect
```

2. Tropical rain forests

For the section on the **tropical rain forests** you will need to revise:

- where the tropical rain forests are located in the world; [📖 *182*]
- what the ecosystem is like in a small area of rain forest; [📖 *182–183*]
- how and why people are destroying the rain forests; [📖 *184–185*]
- what the effects of deforestation are on the people who live in the rain forests and the local environment; [📖 *186–187*]
- how the rain forests can be used in a sustainable way. [📖 *188–191*]

Remember: do not get mixed up between local and global effects of deforestation on the environment. Deforestation can lead to global warming but this is a global effect.

Remember: if resources are used in a sustainable way, they are not being used faster than they can be naturally replenished. Sustainable development allows resources to be used now without destroying them for future generations.

Diagram sequence – deforestation

A sequence of linked boxes (flow diagram) should help you learn about the impacts of chopping down vegetation on soils in areas like Amazonia.

Notice how specialist terms are used here. They are shown in *italics*. If you don't know what they mean, look up their meanings in your textbook or your notes.

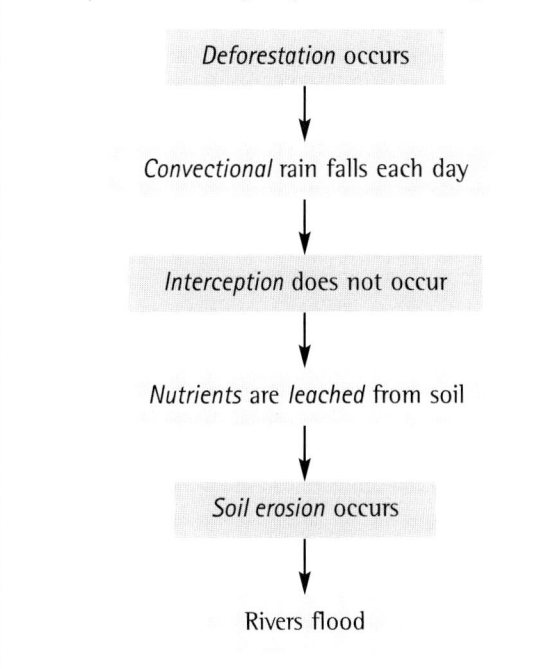

Deforestation occurs
↓
Convectional rain falls each day
↓
Interception does not occur
↓
Nutrients are *leached* from soil
↓
Soil erosion occurs
↓
Rivers flood

People and the Environment

Tasks to do

Try to learn the sequence and produce two more flow diagrams to show the impacts of deforestation on **ecosystems** and **local people**.

3. National Parks

National Parks are areas of beautiful scenery which were set up to conserve the natural beauty and provide opportunities for the public to enjoy the countryside. They are areas where people live and work and the many uses of the land may cause conflict between different groups of people who want to use them in different ways. [192]

> **Remember:** conflict happens when a group of people make use of an area in a way which causes problems for other people who want to make use of the area in a different way.

> **Remember:** a National Park is an area of countryside where people live and work. It is not just a playground for tourists – don't confuse National Parks with theme parks like Alton Towers.

Your case study must be of a National Park in the UK. It should focus on the conflicts which are caused by the land being used for a variety of purposes. The tourist industry does cause many conflicts but you should also know about conflicts which result from:

- mining and quarrying;
- military use;
- forestry;
- water supply;
- agriculture.

Mnemonic – Users of a National Park

When you learn about conflicts over land use in the National Park, which you use as your case study, you could try to use a mnemonic to remember the different land uses.

How about FARM RACE?

Forestry
Army training
Reservoirs
Mining (and quarrying)
Recreation
Agriculture
Conservation
Education

Fact or fiction – National Parks

Look at these statements about National Parks in the UK. Discuss them with a partner and decide which six are fact and which are fiction.

a) All the land is owned by the Government.
b) No new buildings can be built.
c) The first National Parks were set up in the 1950s.
d) The cost of entry is low.
e) National Parks are closed in winter.
f) Most land is privately owned.
g) National Parks are areas which are being preserved.
h) There is no industry in National Parks.
i) There are many opportunities for outdoor leisure activities.
j) Entry to all National Parks is free.
k) People live and work in National Parks.
l) National Parks are areas of scenic beauty.

A New Introduction to Geography for OCR GCSE Specification A: Revision Guide 53

> A good way of showing activities which conflict is to use a 'conflict matrix' such as the one below. It is useful to show not only which activities might possibly conflict, but also which conflicts are most difficult to resolve.
>
> [conflict matrix diagram with categories: Reservoirs for water supply, Quarrying and mining, Military training, Forestry, Farming, Active leisure, e.g. walking, sailing, Passive leisure, e.g. car ride, picnic, Landscape conservation]
>
> Major conflicts are shown by a cross.
> Possible conflicts are shown by a question mark.
> Activities which are in harmony are shown by a tick.
>
> **Can you complete the two missing lines?**
>
> You will also need to know what strategies are being used in your case study example to reduce conflicts, and particularly be able to explain how they can be used in a sustainable way.

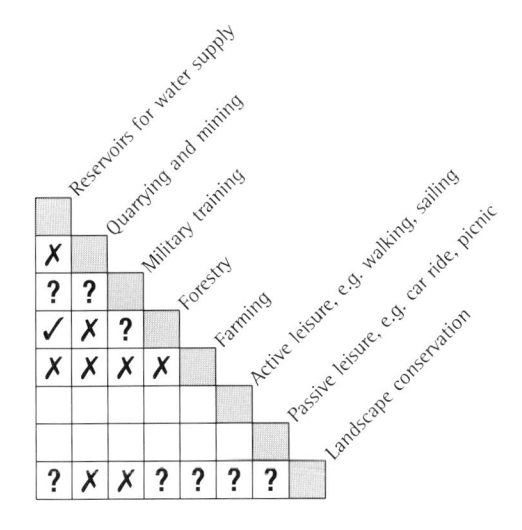

Remember: building and development is not banned in a National Park. It can take place providing planning permission is obtained, but not everyone will agree with it. Make sure that you learn the details of the conflicts which will result from any examples of developments in your case study area.

4. Water pollution

You will need a case study of the causes and effects of water pollution. This can be taken from anywhere in the world and can focus on the pollution of either a river, lake or sea area. It should include information about:

▶ the name and location of the river, lake or sea area.

▶ the causes of the pollution.

▶ the effects of the pollution on people and the natural environment.

▶ what can be done to reduce the likelihood of future pollution. [*196–201*]

Remember: rivers, lakes and seas are always being polluted and you may have seen or read news items about recent incidents. Impress the examiner by your knowledge of a recent event such as a spillage from an oil tanker. By using newspaper articles and websites, you will be able to learn plenty of specific details to write high level case study answers.

GLOBAL ENVIRONMENT

The **global environment** section looks at two different environmental issues:

1. Acid rain

Acid rain is caused by the use of fossil fuels in power stations and vehicles. The polluting gases react with oxygen in the atmosphere to produce dilute acids which fall as rain after being carried by the prevailing winds. You will need to know the following:

▶ the physical processes and human activities which cause acid rain. [*202–203*]

▶ the effects of acid rain on people and the natural environment. [*203–204*]

▶ strategies which can be used to reduce acid rain. In particular you will need to understand why it is important for countries to work together to reduce acid rain. [*204–205*]

You need to be able to give examples from the UK and the EU to illustrate the causes and effects of acid rain.

Remember: acid rain is a global environmental problem because it can affect any part of the world as prevailing winds may carry the acids for up to 2000 kilometres for several days before the rain falls.
You may be able to use some of your case study knowledge from this unit, such as eutrophication, in answering a question about agriculture in Unit 3 (see page 40 of this Revision Guide).

People and the Environment

2. Global warming

Global warming is caused by a build up of greenhouse gases in the atmosphere which results in an increase in the average temperatures of the earth. Whilst greenhouse gases are present naturally in the atmosphere, it is believed that human activities have been responsible for the average temperature increases during the 20th century. You will need to know the following:

- the physical processes and human activities which cause global warming. [206–207]
- the present and potential future consequences of global warming. [207–208]
- strategies which can be used to reduce global warming. Again you must understand why it is important for countries to work together to reduce the emissions of greenhouse gases. [209]

You also need to be able to describe how real places in different parts of the world may be affected in different ways by global warming. Explain why they will be affected in these ways.

> **Remember:** make sure that you know what the difference is between acid rain and global warming and that you learn how emissions of gases can cause different effects. The hole in the ozone layer is another global environmental problem but don't get this mixed up with acid rain and global warming.

A detailed look at questions on the tropical rain forest

Now that you know what you need to learn it is important that you are able to use your knowledge and understanding in the correct way. Look at the resources which have been used for the first part of this question. It is based on the satellite image on the back cover of this book.

You will have used satellite images in your geography lessons. [20 and 199]. One may be used as a resource in your examination. You will be provided with a key to identify the land uses from the colours on the image.

You will be able to see how the examiner has used the satellite image to put together this question on the rain forest. (See Figure 21 on page 55.)

These questions are testing knowledge (K), application (A) and skills (S).

a) The largest settlement on the map is called Manaus. Describe the location of Manaus. (2S)

b) i) Give the coordinates for a square on the satellite image where rain forests have been cleared. (1S)

   ii) Describe the distribution of the land where the rain forest has been cleared. (3S)

   iii) Explain why the rain forest in some areas has been cleared whilst it remains untouched in other areas. (2A)

💡 Words as dominoes – Global environmental problems

Here is a series of words connected with global environmental problems. Copy them out, on oblong cards like dominoes.

Acid rain	Greenhouse effect
Carbon dioxide	International cooperation
Chlorofluorocarbons (CFCs)	Kyoto Summit
Deforestation	Methane
Desulphurisation	Prevailing winds
Drought	Nitrogen oxides
Energy conservation	Radiation
Global warming	Sulphur dioxide

As in the game of dominoes, one player puts a card down and the next player adds a card at either end – but only if he or she can explain the link between the two words they are joining together.

For example these two cards would go together:

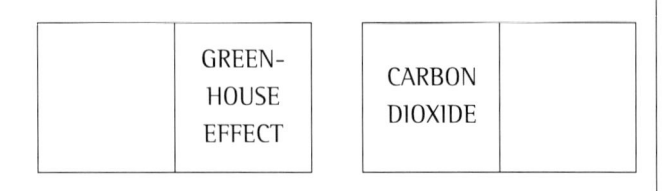

| GREEN-HOUSE EFFECT | CARBON DIOXIDE |

The link is that carbon dioxide is one of the gases which produce the greenhouse effect.

A New Introduction to Geography for OCR GCSE Specification A: Revision Guide   55

FIGURE 21

The area shown on the Satellite image (on the back cover of this book)

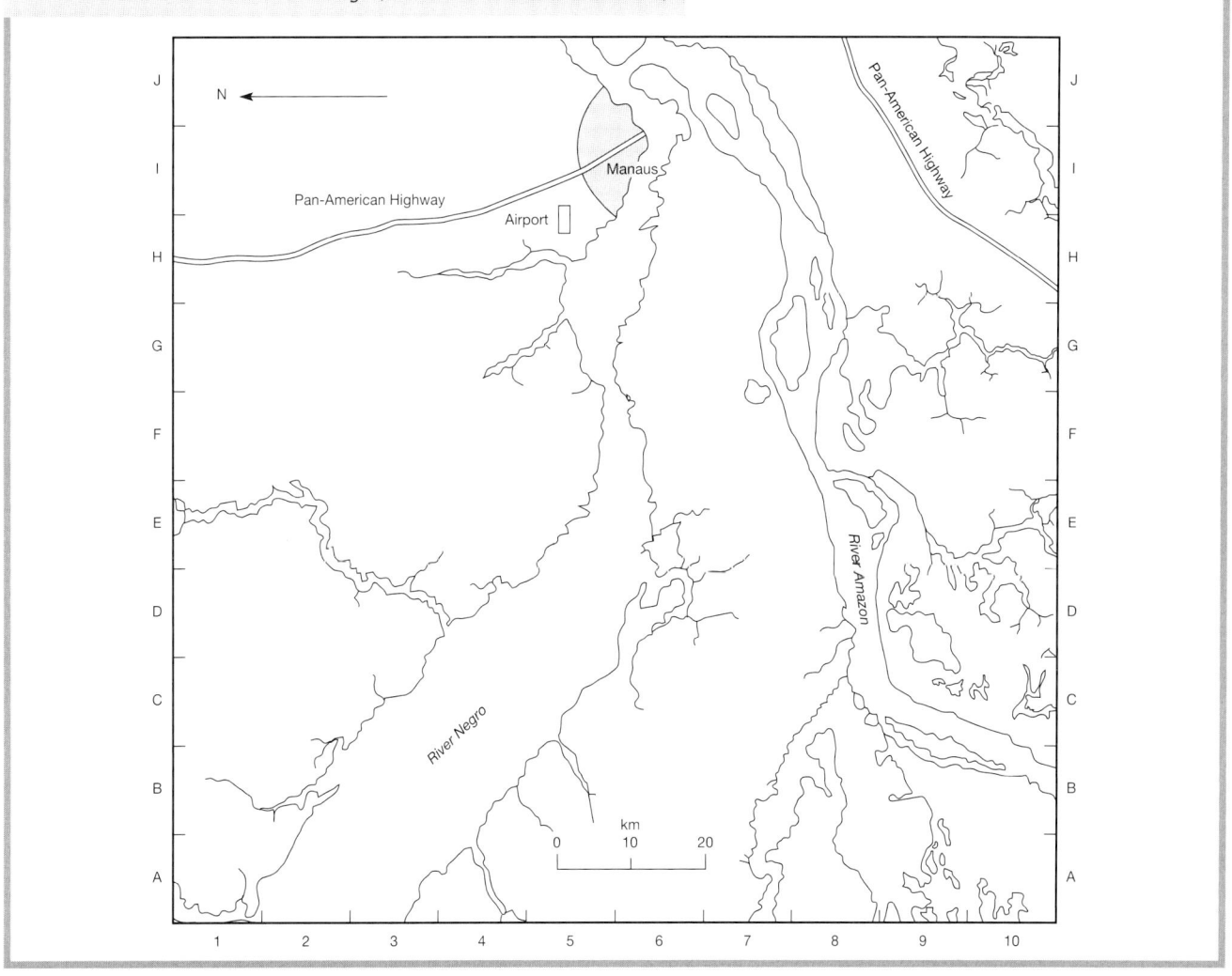

c) i) How does the water in the River Negro differ from that in the River Amazon? (1S)

ii) Suggest reasons why the water in the River Negro differs from that of the River Amazon. (3A)

d) Name a square where some of the tropical rain forest has been cut down. Describe how this has affected the people and local environment.
(7K)

Three sections of this question are directly using the satellite image. Look at the key to discover which colour is used to represent areas where rain forest has been cleared (sections b (i) and (ii) and to find out why areas of water are represented in different colours on the image (section c (i))

Remember: if you are given a satellite image to use you will need to use the key which goes with it to work out how the land is used.

Can you remember how to **describe the location** of a place? If not look back at Unit 2 and then practise this skill by accurately describing the location of Manaus (section a) by using the map. Section b (ii) asks you to '**describe the distribution** of land where rainforest has been cleared'. If you are asked to describe a distribution, you need to be writing about patterns rather than one particular place. Phrases like these are useful when describing a distribution:

- spread out.
- evenly (or unevenly) distributed.
- in lines.
- in the northern/southern/eastern/western part of _____ .
- around the edges of _____ .
- close to the centre of _____ .
- along (away from) the rivers/coast.

Look again at the satellite image and try to use these ideas to describe the distribution of rain forest. Section b (ii) on page 54 is worth three marks. Can you find three points to write about the distribution pattern?

People and the Environment

Remember: to read carefully the **command words** which are used throughout the question. Don't confuse 'describe the location' with 'describe the distribution'.

In part c (ii) on page 55 you need to apply your understanding of what happens when rain forests are cut down, so that you can suggest reasons for the difference in water quality between the Rivers Amazon and Negro. The soil is exposed to the heavy rain when trees are cut down. You should be able to apply your knowledge of the hydrological cycle in Unit 1 to explain why this should affect the quality of the river water in areas close to where trees have been cut down.

The final section of this question is the case study.

Name of case study:
The Amazon Rain Forest

Key idea:
The impacts of cutting down the rain forest on both the people who live in the rain forest and on ecosystems and the natural environment.

Do not write about:
The reasons why trees are being chopped down in the rain forest.
The impacts on the global environment such as global warming.

Ideas to include	
People	Local Environment
How the culture of the local people is affected	What happens to species of trees and plants
Why the survival of local people is threatened	The impacts on food chains in the rain forest
What causes outbreaks of disease	What happens to the soil when trees have been removed
Why many people were homeless and short of food	What happens to wildlife
What causes conflicts between local people and developers	What happens when heavy rain falls
Whether local people can get employment as a result of the development	The effects on rivers in the area

HOW THE CASE STUDY IS MARKED

The mark scheme for this case study question is as follows:

Level 1:
The candidate's answer includes statements with limited detail which describe the effects of cutting down the rain forest.

Level 2:
The candidate's answer includes more developed statements which describe the effects of cutting down the rain forest.

Level 3:
The candidate's answer includes comprehensive and place specific statements which describe the effects of cutting down the rain forest.

Remember: if the question is asking you about the people and the environment, you must try to make several different points about each. To be 'comprehensive', a level 3 answer must include information about both the people and the environment. It must consist of developed, place specific statements.

In both of your examination papers, you will be given a mark for how well you write extended answers, such as case studies. This is referred to as the Quality of Written Communication. You should write as clearly as you can so that the examiner can easily understand the points which you are making. In addition you should use the specialist terms which you have learned in geography wherever you can rather than using everyday language.

On Papers 1 and 2 there are four marks for the Quality of Written Communication. These are awarded using the following levels:

Candidate is able to communicate in written form, though the message is not always clear.

(1 mark)

Candidate communicates clearly by writing brief, simple statements, using everyday language.

(2 marks)

Candidate generally communicates effectively, using specialist terms in some parts of answers.

(3 marks)

Candidate communicates effectively throughout and uses specialist terms where appropriate.

(4 marks)

Tasks to do

Here is a level 3 answer to the case study on the rainforest. It would also be awarded a high mark for the Quality of Written Communication.

Look at the answer and identify where the candidate:

- includes information about both the people who live in the area and the local environment.
- develops the ideas rather than just making simple statements.
- writes about real places rather than describing vague effects.
- uses specialist terms rather than everyday language.

Name an area where the tropical rain forest has been cut down. Describe how this has affected the people and local environment. (7)

Large areas of the Amazon rain forest have been cut down. In the 1980s there was much deforestation in Rondonia to create farmland. When the protective vegetation cover had been removed the heavy convectional rain caused much of the soil to be eroded and leaching to occur. Tribes of Amazonian Indians such as the Erigbaagtsa or the Yanomami who lived in the rain forest were wiped out as they could no longer use it for supplies of food. Many were killed by coming into contact with diseases like flu to which they had no resistance. The soils became very poor after a few years and the new settlers had to move elsewhere as farmland and cattle ranches were abandoned.

When iron ore was mined at Carajas large numbers of trees were removed to dig out the rock. Some of the species found there are rare. It could be that in the rain forests there are cures for AIDS or cancer.

For example, the Periwinkle flower is used to help cure childhood leukaemia. In addition whole ecosystems were threatened as food chains were destroyed. Predators were unable to find food and some species were threatened with extinction.

Remember: use the specialist terms which you have learned in geography lessons whenever you can. Find them in a glossary. [📖 239] Try to learn them all.

Here is another example of a case study question from this unit:

For a river, lake or sea area which you have studied, describe the causes and effects of pollution on people and the natural environment.

Your case study may be a local or a recent one. It could be the pollution of the Guadiamar River in Spain or the oil spillage along the Pembrokeshire coast of Wales. [📖 197–201]

You may be able to add more details to your case study by researching on the Internet. For example, if you have studied the Sea Empress disaster on the Pembrokeshire coast you could look at websites like:

http://www.swan.ac.uk/empress/
http://www.aber.ac.uk/iges/cti-g/STHAZARDS/seaempress/sea.html

Tasks to do

Use either of these case studies, or another example from your notes to try to write a level 3 answer. Remember to achieve level 3, your answers must:

- include several ideas which should be developed, using geographical terms where appropriate.
- include details about real places. In this case, details of the sea area which was polluted and the coastal settlements which were affected.
- be comprehensive. In this case it should include information about both the causes and effects, on both the people and the natural environment.

How to Prepare for Papers 3 and 4

The questions in Papers 3 and 4 are different because they are based on different types of resources. They aim to test what you have understood and can do. They are not testing knowledge and therefore you will not need to learn factual information for these papers. However it is important for you to practise answering the types of question which appear on these papers, and to know how the examiners will be marking your answers. The questions will test:

- understanding – what you can work out.
- application – how you can transfer your understanding to another place or situation.
- skills – whether you can draw or interpret maps, graphs and other resources.

One of the resources is an **Ordnance Survey map**.

This could be 1:25000 or 1:50000 scale.

There are examples of each of these maps inside the covers of this book.

The 1:25000 map shows part of Chester.

The 1:50000 map shows Bath and part of the surrounding area.

Make sure that you are able to:

- find and give 4 figure and 6 figure grid references.
- use the scale accurately to work out distances.
- use the key to work out which features are at points on the map.
- draw a sketch section and locate features onto it.
- describe the location of a settlement or other feature.
- describe and suggest reasons for a distribution.
- plot accurately a feature (e.g. a road, river, lake or settlement) on a sketch map.
- use map evidence to describe features of the landscape and how the area is used by people.

You need to be confident in these skills and make sure that you respond correctly to the command words used. The next exercise uses the 1:50000 map of Bath which is inside the back cover of the book.

Tasks to do

Use the Ordnance Survey map of the Bath area inside the front cover.

- For each question you are given three answers.
- Decide which one is correct.
- Decide which one is wrong because the candidate has not read the question carefully.

1. **Identify** the type of woodland in grid square 6864.
   a. *coniferous.*
   b. *mixed.*
   c. *Corston Field.*

2. **State** the evidence which suggests that Bath is a tourist attraction.
   a. *There are museums and an abbey.*
   b. *Tourists mainly visit Bath in the summer because it is hotter.*
   c. *There are beaches and amusement arcades.*

3. **Name** a village within 1km of the River Avon.
   a. *Corston.*
   b. *Bath.*
   c. *To obtain fresh water.*

4. **Give** a 6 figure reference for a river confluence (where two rivers join).
   a. *625704*
   b. *7062*
   c. *704625*

5. **Describe** the relief of the land in grid square 7161.
   a. *It is gently sloping land between 80 and 160 metres above sea level.*
   b. *It is used for farmland.*
   c. *Relief is the height and shape of the land.*

6. **Suggest two reasons** why the village of Tunley (6959) has few services.

   a. *It has a public house which local people can use. It has a bus service passing through.*

   b. *It is close to Bath where everyone works in the tourist industry. There is not enough room to build shops.*

   c. *It is too small for high order services to be profitable. Many people will use services in Bath where they work.*

7. **Compare** the location of the camping and caravan sites at Stantonbury House (670645) and Clays End (713647.)

   a. *One is nearer to the main road, the A39.*

   b. *The one at Stantonbury House is near to a public house.*

   c. *The one at Clays End is nearer to Bath.*

8. **To what extent** are the Government Offices at 741677 at a good location?

   a. *They are located where there is plenty of space so land will be cheaper, however residents of Bath will need to travel out of the city centre to use them.*

   b. *They are located 4 km to the NNW of the centre of Bath on gently sloping land which is 220 metres above sea level.*

   c. *They are located close to main roads which will make access for workers easy, however the flat land on which they are built is likely to flood easily.*

The Ordnance Survey map will not be the only resource which is used in Papers 3 and 4. Other resources will be used which could include:

- maps of different types (e.g. land use maps, street maps, maps showing the distribution of earthquakes and volcanoes).

- maps at different scales, from the small scale maps of the world to large scale maps, such as the one on page 43, which shows the location of Prolog.

- graphs of different types (e.g. bar graph, pie graph, line graph, divided rectangles, scatter graphs and triangular graphs).

- photographs and satellite images.

- cartoons.

- tables of figures.

Below are some examples of the types of question which use the 1:25000 Ordnance Survey map of Chester, which is inside the back cover of the book, along with three different types of resources:

- a graph

- a cartoon

- photographs

You will notice that the following three questions are all worth 5 or 6 marks. Any question which is worth 5 or 6 marks will be marked using a levels of response mark scheme.

Question 1

FIGURE 22

Number of vehicles using Wrexham Road Park and Ride site in 1999

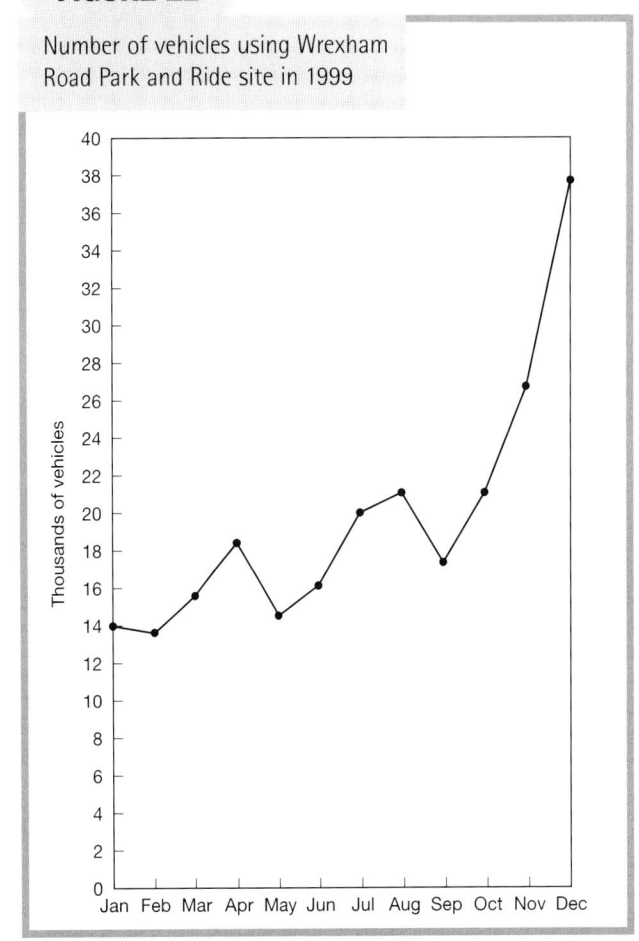

The graph shows the number of vehicles using Wrexham Road Park and Ride car park in 1999.

Describe the trend shown by the graph. Refer to information on the graph in your answer. (5 marks)

How to Prepare for Papers 3 and 4

The line graph is a type of graph which is used to show change over a period of time. This example shows changes in the number of cars using the Park and Ride at Wrexham Road. You should be able to find this on the Ordnance Survey map of Chester at 390630.

This question uses the graph to test your skill of interpretation.

> **Remember:** to locate places on the Ordnance Survey map the examiner will expect you to use grid references. Make sure you can accurately use both 4 and 6 figure references. The grid number along the bottom come first, then the numbers up the side of the map.

Mark scheme

Level 1:
Statements which indicate the general increase during the year.

Level 2:
Statements which show that the increase is not a continuous trend but contains variations.

Level 3:
Statements which support the trend and variations with details from the graph, by referring to number of vehicles and months.

Task to do

With a partner think of some examples of statements at each level. Then each of you attempt to write a level 3 answer. Compare your answers.

> **Remember:** to achieve level 3, your answer must include detailed information from the graph.

Cartoons are sometimes used in questions to test your understanding of an issue. The cartoon illustrates the conflicts which sometimes occur when a by-pass is built around an urban area. If you look again at the Ordnance Survey map of Chester you will find the A55 (T), a by-pass which goes around Chester.

Question 2

Identify the conflicts between different groups of people which are shown by the cartoon. Use map evidence to help you explain why these conflicts occur when a by-pass is built. (6 marks)

Task to do

With a partner work out an answer to this question.

> **Remember:** when you are asked to use map evidence it will help you to achieve level 3 if you give actual examples from the map, using grid references.

Photographs taken in the area shown by the Ordnance Survey map are likely to be used in Papers 3 and 4.

Question 3

Photograph A

Chester CBD

Identify the measures shown in the Photograph A to reduce problems caused by traffic in the CBD of Chester. How successful will these measures be in improving the environment for shoppers and businesses within the CBD? (6 marks)

To reach the highest level you must make sure that you do everything which you are asked to do in the question. You should also aim to include as many ideas as you can and develop the different statements in your answer.

Remember: if the question contains the command 'how successful' it requires you to make a judgement. It suggests that whilst the measures will have helped to reduce problems, they will have only partially improved the CBD for shoppers and businesses.

Mark scheme

Level 1:
The candidate identifies measures which are shown in the photograph to reduce conflict.

Level 2:
The candidate includes more developed statements which suggest how the measures help to reduce conflicts.

Level 3:
The candidate gives a detailed answer, including developed statements, which gives a judgement on the success of the measures shown.

Below are three answers, one at each level. Notice how the answer improves from level 1 to level 3.

Level 1 answer

The following measures are shown in the photograph:
- *Posts have been put up to stop traffic going straight on.*
- *The area has been made into a pedestrian only zone.*
- *Double yellow lines will stop drivers parking.*
- *There is a cycle rack to park bikes so that people won't ride them in the town centre.*

Examiner comment

Notice that this candidate has just listed what has been done in the area. There is no attempt to develop the points in order to explain how the measures will help reduce the problems so the answer will not reach level 2. Even though more than two measures have been listed, this answer will not score more than two marks as it is not answering the question fully.

Level 2 answer

The photograph shows that posts have been put up to stop traffic going into the CBD. The street is now all pavement so that it is much easier for shoppers to walk without worrying about cars and lorries. It will be much safer for pedestrians to go from shop to shop with no cars around. The double yellow lines should stop people parking here and causing a traffic jam. Also the roundabout lets drivers turn round easily. Even people on bikes cannot go into the town centre so there is a cycle rack to fasten their bikes to.

Examiner comment

This is a much more developed answer. For each measure identified, it is suggested how it will help to reduce the problems so the answer has reached level 2. However the answer does not say how successful any of the measures would be but assumes they would work. This answer needs to include a judgement of their likely success to reach level 3.

How to Prepare for Papers 3 and 4

Photograph B

Chester's out of town shopping area

Level 3 answer

In Chester CBD a number of measures have been taken to improve the environment. Posts have been put up to stop traffic going into the CBD so that people can walk more safely from shop to shop. This is a good idea and will encourage more people to go into the town centre. This has created a pedestrian only area where people will be less stressed, as there are no cars to worry about. However, it may make it difficult for old people or those who cannot walk very easily as they may have to carry heavy bags back to their car. It will also make it difficult for delivery lorries to get to the shops.

Yellow lines have been painted on the side of the road to stop people parking. However, as the photograph shows, some people ignore them and park there anyway so they might still block the traffic. Overall I think that the environment will be made better for shoppers as there will be less car exhausts and noise from vehicles which may encourage more people to shop, this will also benefit the businesses.

Examiner comment

This is an excellent answer. It suggests how each measure will help to reduce the problems and makes a very clear judgement about the success of the methods. Remember the question, 'how successful', suggests that the measures will not have completely solved the problems and this answer recognises that this is the case.

Another way in which you may be asked to use your judgement is through the command 'to what extent'.

Look at the following question which refers to Photograph A – *Chester CBD* (taken at grid reference 406661) and Photograph B – *out of town shopping area* (taken at grid reference 390670)

Question 4

To what extent will a shopping development like the one shown in Photograph B affect a town centre shopping area such as that shown in Photograph A? You should develop the points which you make.

The mark scheme is shown below.

> Level 1:
> Simple statements which identify an effect on the CBD and include limited detail, e.g. attracts customers away from town centre, town centre shops lose money.
>
> Level 2:
> More detailed and developed statements which identify effects on the CBD. Candidates could either develop their reasoning (e.g. attracts customers away from town centre as the CBD has limited parking space) or to elaborate upon the effects themselves (e.g. town centre shops lose money and some shops will go out of business).
>
> Level 3:
> Comprehensive and accurate response which includes reference to arguments that the town centre is still likely to survive (e.g. people without cars may still use CBD, specialist shops in CBD will still survive as the new development will not contain such shops).

Task to do

The following answers all achieved level 3, but they have different qualities. Use the mark scheme to identify what makes each answer worth level 3.

Answer 1

A shopping development like in Photograph B will draw business away from a town centre shopping area because it is easy to get to for both city centre dwellers and out of town shoppers. It is also a place where you can get lots of different commodities whilst not walking around much, unlike a town centre.

Parking is easier around an out of town shopping centre because there is more space set aside for it, and in the town centre there is not as much room for large shops or vegetation, making the area less attractive.

On the other hand many shops in out of town shopping centres are shops for commodities that you do not buy very often (e.g. computers) while many people will still go to the town centre areas for specialist shops (e.g. tailors) or for bread and milk, as it is nearer.

In conclusion, Photograph B will take away business from town centre retail areas for a lot of purchases (e.g. a sofa) while areas like in Photograph A will still be in demand for specialist skilled items (a custom suit or one-off table for example).

Answer 2

The shopping centre in Photograph B would affect the town centre area in A. This is because Area B is located outside the centre where land price would be low so the building costs would be low. This would mean that they would be able to offer low prices for goods so therefore more people would buy goods from Area B than the town centre. Therefore town centre shops would lose money. However the shops in Area B sell goods that would not need to be bought often so therefore people would still buy everyday goods from the town centre.

Also tourists visit Chester and would want to buy souvenirs and gifts so these people would still shop in the town centre. They would not want to visit the shops in Area B they may have them in their local area.

People without cars would still shop in the town centre because it is quite difficult to travel to Area B.

The shops in the town centre would be affected by the shops in Area B but not very much as they would still have many customers.

Answer 3

People will probably go to the shopping centre at B because there are lots of well-known shops which are modern and nice to shop in. They will be away from the congestion of the town centre and it will be easier to get to. Also there is plenty of parking which is probably free. So less people will go shopping in the town centre and businesses may lose money and will shut down because there is not enough customers to keep them going. This is bad for the town centre as less people go to shops which stay open.

Some shops will always stay in the town centre so people will still go there. People without a car or who rely on buses like old people will carry on shopping in the town centre. Many town centres are also attractive for shoppers with plenty of entertainment and cafes for shoppers.

There are several questions where you will just have to use the Ordnance Survey map, without any other resource. Here are some examples which use the Chester map.

Question 5

Complete the sketch section along grid line 63 of the map. (5 marks)

Question 6

Mark with an arrow and label on your sketch section the position of Chester Business Park. (1 mark)

How to Prepare for Papers 3 and 4

Remember: a sketch section is a scale drawing of the view from the side if a cut had been made through the land surface. In order to show relief features more clearly, the vertical scale is exaggerated.

Tasks to do:

Check that you are able to draw a reasonably accurate sketch section. Practise this important skill by making a copy and completing the sketch section along grid line 63 of the Chester map. Mark the position of Chester Business Park on your sketch section, along with any other features such as the Park and Ride, the A483 and A55 (T), areas of woodland and the River Dee.

You will have noticed Chester Business Park on the Ordnance Survey map. You may be asked to answer questions such as Questions 7 and 8 that follow:

Question 7

Use evidence from the Ordnance Survey map to describe the site and situation of Chester Business Park. (5 marks)

Remember: 'site' and 'situation' have different meanings. Site refers to the actual piece of land on which the business park is built. Situation refers to the position of the business park in relation to the surrounding area.

Question 8

Suggest reasons for the location of Chester Business Park. (6 marks)

Remember: Question 7 is testing your map reading skills and Question 8 is testing application of your understanding.

Both of these questions about Chester Business Park are marked in levels. To reach the highest level, you would need to develop the points which you make and give evidence from the map. Questions 9 and 10 will help you improve your answers to Questions 7 and 8.

Tasks to do

Write paragraphs to answer Questions 9 and 10 by developing these short sentences. Use the ideas in brackets to help you develop the points.

FIGURE 23

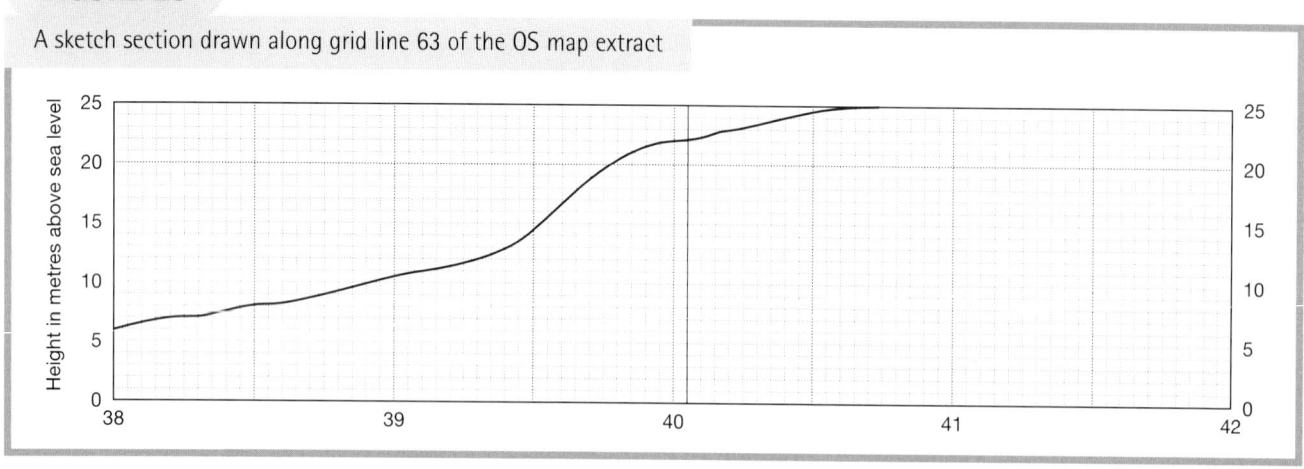

A sketch section drawn along grid line 63 of the OS map extract

Question 9

Use evidence from the Ordnance Survey map to describe the site and situation of Chester Business Park.

The Business Park is built on a big area of flat land.

(What is the height of the land on which it is built? What is the approximate area of the Business Park?)

It is outside Chester.

(What compass direction is it from the centre of Chester? How far is it from the centre of Chester and from the suburban housing areas?)

It is near the roundabout

(Which roundabout? What are the numbers of the main roads which meet at this roundabout? How close is it to the roundabout and which compass direction from it?)

Question 10

Suggest reasons for the location of Chester Business Park.

It is near Chester.

(Why is this important? – think about availability of a workforce.)

It is useful to be near a main road.

(Why is a location close to a main road important? – think about the transport of materials and finished products and access for workers and customers.)

The land is easy to build on.

(What is it which makes it easy to build on? – think about the relief of the land and the space for buildings, parking and possible future expansion.)

It is a location in an area of countryside.

(Why is this appealing when locating a business park? – think about the attractions of the environment and landscape to the workforce and give examples from the map. How will the cost of this large area of land compare with the cost of a similar amount of land nearer to the centre of Chester?)

Another style of question to test understanding and application is to consider the advantages and disadvantages of a particular development.

> **Remember:** there are other ways to refer to advantages and disadvantages, such as benefits and problems, or ideas in favour or against.

How to Prepare for Papers 3 and 4

Now test your skills of interpreting and understanding different resources. Then apply your understanding to see both sides of the issue.

Question 11

Suggest the advantages and disadvantages of living in the Isle of Dogs area. Give evidence from the map and photographs in your answer.

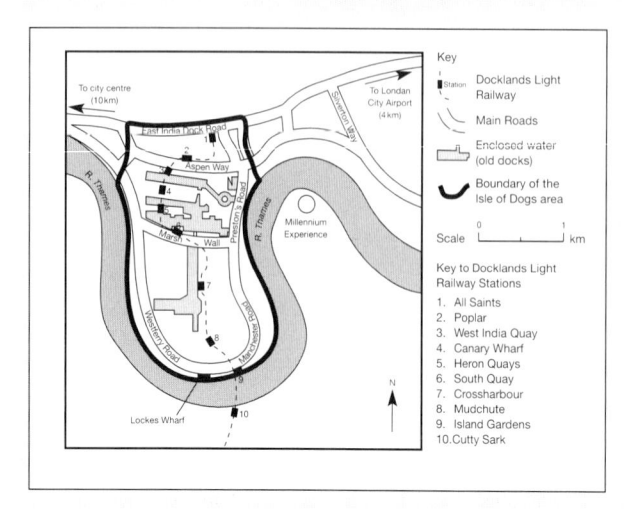

Mark scheme

Level 1
Simple statements identifying advantages and/or disadvantages of living in the Isle of Dogs area which include limited detail. (e.g. it will be noisy. There is a lot of traffic. It is easy to get into Central London. There are lots of jobs.)

Level 2
More detailed and developed statements identifying advantages and/or disadvantages of living in the Isle of Dogs area. (e.g. There will be noise from traffic/construction sites. Heavy traffic will cause danger to young children. It is easy to get into Central London by public transport/where work is available in service sector etc.)

Level 3
Comprehensive and accurate response which includes reference to both advantages and disadvantages, quoting evidence from the maps and photographs. (e.g. There will be noise from the construction site at Lockes Wharf. Heavy traffic using the Westferry Road will cause danger to young children. It is easy to get into Central London by using the Docklands Light Railway with several stations such as Herons Quays and Canary Wharf.)

Remember: in this type of question you need to consider both sides of the arguments, i.e. advantages and disadvantages, in order to produce a level 3 answer.

Task to do

Below are three answers to this question. Decide which answer fits each of levels 1, 2 and 3. Upon what evidence have you based your decision?

Answer 1

The disadvantages of living in the Isle of Dogs are that there will be a lot of disturbing noises from the construction sites. This noise pollution can be uncomfortable to live near whilst it is taking place. Another problem is that there will be a lot of traffic congestion and pollution as people go to work in the big offices.

On the other hand the advantages may be that people who live here can easily get to work in central London via the many train stations on the Docklands Light Railway or the main roads such as East India Dock Road. The luxury apartments and town houses at Locke Wharfe may improve the attractiveness of the area and these buildings give a pleasant view of the River Thames.

Answer 2

Benefits of living in the Isle of Dogs area include the fact that there is a wide variety of jobs nearby in offices and tourism. It is close to London where many people will want to work. It is a modern area so there will be many places of entertainment to visit.

Problems with living in the area include the fact that there may be a problem with traffic and congestion on the roads as the area is very built-up with many places of work which attract people with cars. There can be problems of conflict between visitors and local people through traffic and noise pollution from vehicles which will be high in the area.

Answer 3

One problem of living in the Isle of Dogs is that it could be noisy for people who live there. There are no cafes or restaurants for workers to get lunch etc. and there are other industry buildings nearby.

However, there are advantages such as it is built next to a main road to London and next to railway stations for access. It is on the outskirts of town so not much pollution affects the people living in the Isle of Dogs.

The resources in the examination paper can suggest someone's point of view. They could be showing you an area where change is proposed or a decision has been made which is not popular with everyone. Begin by thinking who will benefit or be in favour. Then think who will be against the proposal or who will be worse off. For each, look carefully at the resources for the evidence. It may be a source of employment, so if it were closed, local people would lose their jobs. It may be smoke from a chimney suggesting pollution. It may be a scheme which is possible but the money would benefit more people if it were spent on other things.

If you can see a situation where someone is likely to be in favour for one reason and the same person is likely to oppose the same thing for a different reason, you really are seeing both sides of the argument!

Question 12

Suggest the likely arguments in favour and against schemes to control coastal erosion of the Holderness coast around Mappleton. Develop the points you make by reference to evidence from the maps and photographs on page 68. [48–51]

Question 13

What benefit and problems might the quarry and works cause for people living in the surrounding settlements and for tourists? Refer to evidence from the resources on page 89 in your answer. [230 and 237]

Tasks to do

Questions 12 and 13 tell you to consider different points of view. To answer these questions you might start with a plan which includes tables like the ones below.

Mappleton

In favour of coastal protection scheme	Against coastal protection scheme

Quarry near Castleton

Benefits of the quarry and works	Problems caused by the quarry and works

Draw your own tables to put in your ideas. Remember you will need to develop these ideas with details from the resources to score higher level marks.

How to Prepare for Papers 3 and 4

FIGURE 25

Mappleton in 1910

Mappleton in 1988

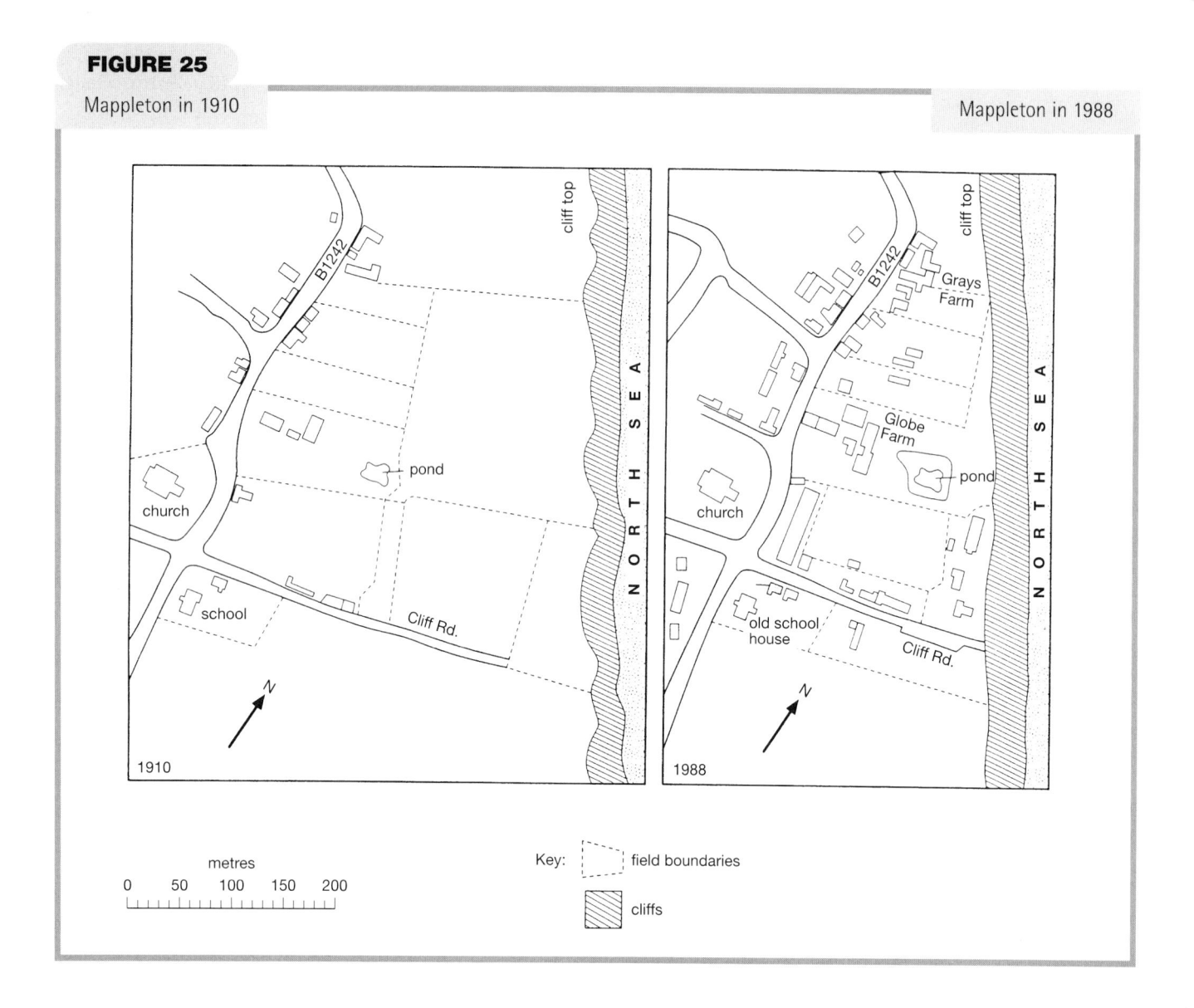

Key: field boundaries / cliffs

metres 0 50 100 150 200

FIGURE 26

Cliff top farm south of Mappleton

FIGURE 27

Coastal defences at Mappleton

A New Introduction to Geography for OCR GCSE Specification A: Revision Guide 69

FIGURE 28

A quarry near Castleton

FIGURE 30

Reasons for visiting National Parks

	Reason %
Scenery/landscape	61
Enjoyed earlier visit	37
Easy to get to	33
Peace and quiet	28
Outdoor activity	18
Event/attraction	16
As it is a National Park	15
Come every year	9
Visit friends/family	5
Own accomodation in area	4
Other	20

FIGURE 29

Peak Park economy: jobs and workforce

In the Peak District National Park
37 000 residents
16 000 workers
19 600 jobs
(12 800 full time)
(5 065 part time)
(1 823 seasonal)

In the surrounding lowlands
8 000 workers

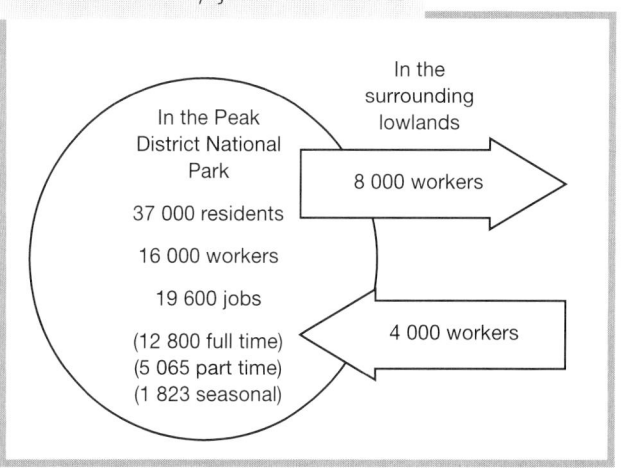

4 000 workers

FIGURE 31

Peace and quiet in the National Park?

Checklist

CHECKLIST

☐ Are you entered for Foundation or Higher Tier?

☐ What date is your first Geography exam?

☐ What day of the week is that?

☐ Is it a morning or an afternoon exam?

☐ How long does the first exam last?

☐ What date is your second Geography exam?

☐ What day of the week is that?

☐ Is it a morning or an afternoon exam?

☐ How long does the second exam last?

☐ Do you have a blue or black pen? (No other ink colour allowed!)

☐ Do you have a spare pen?

☐ Have you remembered your ruler for measuring from maps and completing graphs?

☐ Do you have a calculator in case you need it?

☐ Do you have a sharp pencil?

☐ Do you have a rubber?

☐ Do you have coloured pencils?

☐ Is your pencil case transparent?

☐ Do you have confidence because you have revised thoroughly?